WELCOME

A huddle of humbled Nazi leaders in a simple schoolhouse, a pair of ominous and destructive mushroom clouds and an awesome assemblage of military strength in the home waters of a once mighty foe now vanquished – these are indelible images of the decisive drama of World War Two. After six long years, the greatest armed conflict in the history of man finally came to an end in 1945.

With the demise of Adolf Hitler and his henchmen, the full horror of Nazi atrocities and crimes against humanity was being exposed to the world, while the extent of Japanese brutality in the Far East was sharply coming into focus. Concentration camps were liberated by the Western Allies and the surging Red Army that would soon come to control virtually all of eastern Europe. Human skeletons emerged from the depths of fetid jungle work camps, the mines and the factories of the Japanese home islands, having survived, incredibly, the privations of imprisonment, torture and slave labour.

As the Allied triumph over the dark Axis vision of global domination became inevitable, there was a glimmer of hope for the future. While the perpetrators of heinous crimes were rounded up and put on trial in numerous venues, the charter of the United Nations was created in the hopes of avoiding another cataclysmic clash of arms. For better or worse, the organisation survives today as a forum for international discourse.

Amid the ruin and rubble of war's devastation, there were millions displaced, millions more made destitute and millions more dead, some estimates of the lost reaching 85 million civilian and military personnel. Man's inhumanity to man was starkly made known in images so shocking they could scarcely be believed. When General Dwight D Eisenhower, Supreme Allied commander in the West, witnessed the human calamity of the Ohrdruf concentration camp for himself, he required the local townspeople to tour the spectre of Dante's Inferno made reality – lest such acts be forgotten or repeated.

In 1945, the world was at war and then found itself grappling with peace and a new order. For much of the year there was unfinished business. Forces of the German Wehrmacht fought like lions in defence

Soldiers of the US 255th Infantry Regiment pick their way through the rubble of the once picturesque German town of Waldenburg. (US Army via Wikimedia Commons)

of their homeland, squeezed in the iron vice of Allied spearheads from both East and West. The armed forces of Imperial Japan, living and dying by their code of Bushido, regularly fought to the death. Across the Pacific, fanatical resisters were burned, blasted or entombed in caves and tunnels on embattled islands. They were lost in Kamikaze plunges and the battered hulks of their warships. Even in the last hours, heroes gave their lives for freedom, and villains were meted retribution on the battlefield until the guns finally fell silent.

The fighting ended in Europe and in the Pacific with last violent convulsions. These clashes and more are remembered in the pages of *WORLD WAR TWO: 1945*. Welcome! Come and explore the year of tremendous transformation – 1945.

Left: Top, German officers sign the unconditional surrender in Reims, France. Bottom, Allied force leaders at the signing, May 7, 1945. (US National Archives and Records Administration)

Right: General Tomoyuki Yamashita, 'Tiger of Malaya', leads his staff to surrender on the Philippine island of Luzon. (US National Archives and Records Administration via Wikimedia Commons)

CONTENTS

Katyusha rockets light up the sky during Red Army offensive operations on the Eastern Front in January 1945. (Government of the Russian Federation via Wikimedia Commons)

Troops of the US 101st Airborne Division leave Bastogne, Belgium, after their heroic defence of the town during the Battle of the Bulge. (US Army via Wikimedia Commons)

British soldiers march through the streets of Berlin during the large military parade of July 21, 1945. (Collections of the Imperial War Museums via Wikimedia Commons)

Red Army soldiers celebrate the fall of Berlin with song and dance, May 1945. (Creative Commons Bundesarchiv Bild via Wikimedia Commons)

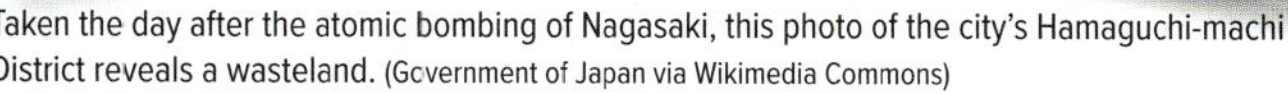

Taken the day after the atomic bombing of Nagasaki, this photo of the city's Hamaguchi-machi District reveals a wasteland. (Government of Japan via Wikimedia Commons)

A session of the Allied International Military Tribunal for the Far East convenes in Tokyo. (US Army via Wikimedia Commons)

ISBN: 978 1 83632 177 4
Editor: Mike Haskew
Senior editor, specials: Roger Mortimer
Email: roger.mortimer@keypublishing.com
Cover Design: Steve Donovan
Design: SJmagic DESIGN SERVICES, India
Advertising Sales Manager: Sam Clark
Email: sam.clark@keypublishing.com
Tel: 01780 755131
Advertising Production: Becky Antoniades
Email: Rebecca.antoniades@keypublishing.com

SUBSCRIPTION/MAIL ORDER
Key Publishing Ltd, PO Box 300, Stamford, Lincs, PE9 1NA
Tel: 01780 480404
Subscriptions email: subs@keypublishing.com
Mail Order email: orders@keypublishing.com

Website: www.keypublishing.com/shop

PUBLISHING
Group CEO: Adrian Cox
Publisher: Steve O'Hara

Published by
Key Publishing Ltd, PO Box 100, Stamford, Lincs, PE9 1XQ
Tel: 01780 755131 **Website:** www.keypublishing.com

PRINTING
Precision Colour Printing Ltd, Haldane, Halesfield 1, Telford, Shropshire. TF7 4QQ

DISTRIBUTION
Seymour Distribution Ltd, 2 Poultry Avenue, London, EC1A 9PU
Enquiries Line: 02074 294000.

BATTLE OF THE BULGE RAGES

In the opening hours of the Battle of the Bulge, German troops sprint across a road littered with abandoned American vehicles and equipment. (US National Archives and Records Administration via Wikimedia Commons)

After two weeks of heavy fighting, Allied forces stabilised and began to reverse the gains made by the German onslaught that resulted in the famed Battle of the Bulge. Adolf Hitler's last desperate gamble in the West, Operation Watch on the Rhine had been intended to swiftly penetrate the thin American line in the Ardennes Forest, press panzer spearheads to the crossings of the River Meuse and seize the deepwater port of Antwerp, Belgium. In doing so, Hitler's forces would drive a wedge between the Allied 12th and 21st Army Groups, potentially rupture the sometimes-tenuous Anglo-American alliance and perhaps even achieve a separate peace. In turn, Hitler intended to subsequently transfer forces to the Eastern Front, where the Soviet Red Army was poised to launch an offensive across the River Vistula and strike directly into the Fatherland.

Unleashing 275,000 troops, hundreds of tanks and 2,000 artillery pieces in three armies – the Sixth Panzer under SS General Josef 'Sepp' Dietrich in the north, Fifth Panzer under General Hasso von Manteuffel in the centre and Seventh Army under General Erich Brandenberger in the south – the Germans struck on a 60-mile front from Monschau, Germany, to the town of Echternach in Luxembourg. Initially, Hitler's westward thrust met with success, taking the Americans by surprise and capturing thousands of prisoners.

However, pockets of stiff resistance slowed the German advance, throwing the critical timetable off. Along Elsenborn Ridge on the north shoulder of the German salient, the US 99th Infantry Division clung stubbornly to defensive positions and slackened Dietrich's progress to a crawl until troops were shifted south to outflank the Americans in critical defensive positions around the Schnee Eiffel, a cluster of villages and forested hills that fronted the ridge. Two entire regiments of the US 106th Division were cut off and forced to surrender.

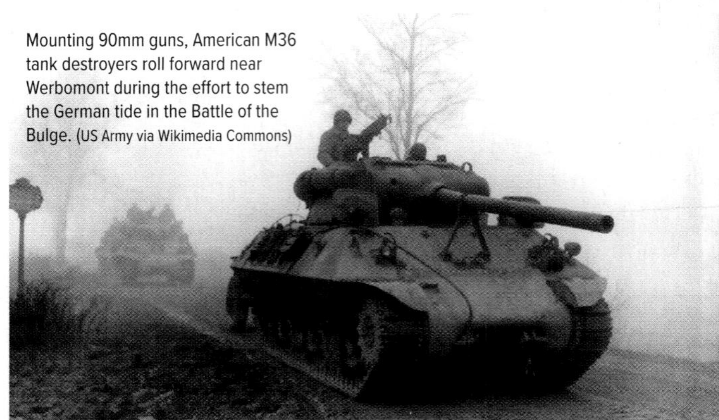

Mounting 90mm guns, American M36 tank destroyers roll forward near Werbomont during the effort to stem the German tide in the Battle of the Bulge. (US Army via Wikimedia Commons)

Dietrich's armoured spearhead, led by the ruthless SS Colonel Joachim Peiper, raced toward vital river crossings, but an intrepid handful of US combat engineers wired critical bridges across the River Ambleve at the town of Stavelot in Belgium, while several spans were blown up literally in the faces of the Germans. Trucked to critical positions around the Belgian town of Werbomont, the 82nd Airborne Division fought tenaciously too, exacting a toll on the attackers.

Peiper had struck with 4,000 troops, but beset by fuel shortages and mounting casualties he was eventually surrounded and forced to retire. Only 800 men in his command managed to escape. In the event, Peiper earned lasting infamy with the massacre of American prisoners in a desolate field near the town of Malmedy, Belgium. Along with several others under his command, Peiper later stood trial for war crimes.

An American soldier escorts a German prisoner to a rear area. Note the German's destroyed PzKpfw V Panther medium tank. (US Army Signal Corps via Wikimedia Commons)

The strain of battle is apparent on the face of this German soldier during the fighting in the Ardennes. (US Government via Wikimedia Commons)

Meanwhile, in the south, Brandenberger's Seventh Army ran directly into the veterans of the US 4th Infantry and 9th Armored Divisions, making virtually no progress. As the Americans clung to Elsenborn Ridge in the north, a distinctive bulge had developed and the momentum of the German penetration ebbed.

In the centre, Manteuffel's tanks came closest to reaching the Meuse before their advance stalled at Dinant, Belgium, about 50 miles from their jump-off point. For six days, elements of the US 7th Armored Division mounted a heroic defence at St Vith, Belgium; they did not capitulate until December 23. At the same time, the Allied high command made tactical adjustments, giving Field Marshal Bernard Montgomery, commander of the 21st Army Group, charge of all forces north of the bulge. Montgomery strengthened his positions in preparation for a decisive counterthrust.

The defence of the crossroads town of Bastogne, Belgium, doomed the German offensive. The Americans' 101st Airborne Division, Combat Command B of the 10th Armored Division and elements of several other units held fast, denying the use of the roads to the Germans. Manteuffel's armoured spearheads reached the town on December 17 and failed to carry the defences by frontal assault. While some German units bypassed the town, others encircled the defenders and demanded their surrender.

Brigadier General Anthony McAuliffe, who led the artillery component of the 101st Airborne Division, was in temporary command while General Maxwell Taylor was away in Washington DC. His response to the surrender demand issued on December 22 has been enshrined among wartime communiques. He simply retorted: "Nuts!"

After holding a woodland position all night near Wiltz, Luxembourg, against German counterattack, three men of B Company, 101st Engineers, emerge for a rest, January 1945. (US National Archives and Records Administration via Wikimedia Commons)

A soldier of the US 11th Armored Division reaches from an M8 armoured car to shake hands with comrades of the 84th Infantry Division at Houffalize, Belgium, January 1945. (US Government via Wikimedia Commons)

Assessing the situation, General George S Patton, commander of the US Third Army, ordered a 90° pivot, disengaging from offensive operations in the Saar, to rapidly move northward in an epic relief of the embattled Bastogne defenders. The US 4th Armored Division made contact with outposts of the 101st Airborne on the day after Christmas, ending the siege of Bastogne.

By January 1, 1945, the failure of the German offensive had become a foregone conclusion. Once the thrust had been contained, the Allies made the most of opportunities to reduce the bulge and cut off the retreat of enemy troops, many of whom had abandoned their vehicles due to lack of fuel. At mid-month, Allied troops converged on the town of Houffalize in Belgium, effectively erasing the German gains.

The Battle of the Bulge was the largest and costliest in American military history with 80,000 casualties, including more than 8,400 killed, 46,000 wounded and 20,000-plus captured. The German losses were devastating and irreplaceable – 120,000 killed, wounded or taken prisoner, while scores of tanks and other armoured vehicles had been lost, crippling the Nazi war effort in the final days of the Third Reich.

OPERATION NORDWIND

Within a week of its inception, Hitler's Ardennes Offensive had begun to falter. However, the Führer was not ready to admit defeat and proposed another operation in support of the drive toward Antwerp. In the south, Hitler initiated Operation Nordwind (North Wind), an attack against the stationary positions of the US Seventh and French First Armies.

When the Allied response to the German assault to the north expanded to involve a thrust of the US Third Army north from the Saar to relieve the surrounded town of Bastogne, Belgium, the US Sixth Army Corps, under General Jacob Devers, had been obliged to stretch its lines in the south, covering the Rhineland-Palatinate and the provinces of Alsace and Lorraine. Short of replacements and in need of resupply as resources had been transferred to shore up defences in the Ardennes, General Alexander Patch, commanding the Seventh Army, knew that another German attack was likely.

Indeed, Hitler convened his generals at his Eagle's Nest retreat in Bavaria and ordered the start of Nordwind with the coming of the new year of 1945. The offensive would exploit the weakness of the Seventh Army and French First Army defences, inflicting heavy casualties, and moving rapidly to capture the French city of Strasbourg. Success in Nordwind would set the stage for another offensive, Operation Dentist, aimed at the vulnerable rear of the Third Army.

To accomplish the task, the Germans assigned two formations, Army Group Upper Rhine, commanded by Reichsführer SS Heinrich Himmler, and Army Group G, under Colonel General Johannes Blaskowitz. Himmler was no military man, and his lack of strategic and tactical acumen contributed to the eventual failure of Nordwind.

The German offensive began with an artillery barrage on the night of December 31, 1944, and a three-pronged ground advance followed with 17 divisions engaged by the middle of January. Among these were the 21st Panzer, 25th Panzergrenadier, 17th SS Panzergrenadier, and 6th SS Mountain Divisions. Advancing through rugged terrain, 21st Panzer attempted to sever the supply and communication lines into Strasbourg but encountered heavy resistance from the US 79th and 42nd Infantry Divisions, as well as the 14th Armored Division. Elsewhere, elements of the US VI Corps, including the 45th, 63rd and 100th Infantry Divisions along with the 12th Armored Division, were engaged on three sides.

Two weeks of savage fighting stretched into mid-month as the adversaries fought for control of villages in the foothills of the Vosges Mountains. At length, General Dwight Eisenhower, Supreme Allied

US M4 Sherman medium tanks of the 714th Tank Battalion advance during efforts to beat back German advances in Alsace-Lorraine. (US Army via Wikimedia Commons)

Teenage German soldiers of the Waffen-SS surrender to the Allies as Operation Nordwind fades away. (US Army via Wikimedia Commons)

Commander in the West, grew concerned with the losses sustained by the Seventh Army and dispatched reinforcements southward as Allied forces wrested the initiative from the Germans in the Battle of the Bulge. By January 25, Operation Nordwind had been halted and the Germans had suffered another serious defeat, with more than 22,000 casualties.

A German PzKpfw V Panther medium tank advances through obstacles of the Siegfried Line during the Operation Nordwind advance. (Creative Commons Bundesarchiv Bild via Wikimedia Commons)

OPERATION BODENPLATTE

The foul winter weather that cloaked Hitler's Ardennes Offensive prior to being unleashed on December 16, 1944, grounded Allied air power and prevented early interdiction of German armoured spearheads in their drive toward Antwerp. However, the conditions worked against the Nazis, too. An all-out Luftwaffe strike against airfields on the continent was intended to cripple the Allied ability to interfere with ground operations once the weather inevitably cleared.

Therefore, Operation Bodenplatte, or Base Plate, was postponed for two weeks until January 1, 1945. In the event, 900 Luftwaffe fighters would take off from their airfields guided by Junkers Ju-88 night fighters to their targets and destroy as many Allied aircraft on the ground as possible while also shooting up the airfield facilities, aiming to render them inoperable for some time.

Operation Bodenplatte was indeed a surprise – many Allied pilots were going about their morning routines, executing predesignated missions of their own, or sleeping off the effects of new year's celebrations that had stretched into the night. However, the air offensive was a disaster for the Luftwaffe. Rather than striking a paralysing blow to Allied air power, the sorties led to heavy casualties among the German pilots, as well as the loss of many irreplaceable aircraft, and hastened the demise of the Nazi air force that had once dominated the skies over western Europe.

As Allied ground forces advanced after D-Day, much of their tactical air support moved from bases in Britain into France and the Low Countries, maximising the range of the fighter-bombers and reconnaissance aircraft in support of offensive operations. One of these fields, designated B-61, at St Denijs-Westrem near Ghent, Belgium, was home to the four squadrons of No. 131 Wing, Royal Air Force.

Right: Luftwaffe ace Major Günther Specht (left), one of a relatively few experienced German pilots, was killed in action during Operation Bodenplatte. (Creative Commons Bundesarchiv Bild via Wikimedia Commons)

St Denijs was one of 17 such Allied installations targeted for Luftwaffe attack on that particular morning. By then, it was hoped that the success of Bodenplatte would reinvigorate the German ground momentum of the Ardennes Offensive, better known as the Battle of the Bulge, which had already begun to falter.

The experience at St Denijs is representative of the air encounters that took place on January 1, 1945. The three fighter-bomber squadrons based there completed bombing missions against targets in the Netherlands and, as they approached to land, the pilots were shocked to find B-61 under attack by swarms of Luftwaffe fighters. They engaged without hesitation and dogfights swirled across the sky. Meanwhile, installations went up in flames while Supermarine Spitfire fighters that were parked on the ground were shredded.

Even as they fought tenaciously, the Luftwaffe pilots had already taken serious losses. German anti-aircraft batteries along their flightpaths had not been alerted that Bodenplatte was under way, and the gunners had not seen such a concentration of Luftwaffe aircraft in some time; they assumed the airplanes were Allied, opened fire and shot down many of their own aircraft. Further, attrition had claimed the lives of many experienced Luftwaffe pilots before 1945. The pilots who climbed into the cockpits of Messerschmitt Me-109 and Focke Wulf Fw-190 fighters to execute Bodenplatte were young in many cases – they were no match for veteran Allied pilots and their lack of experience was readily apparent.

Without doubt, Bodenplatte was costly for the Allies with 305 aircraft destroyed and 190 damaged, as well as several airfields temporarily out of action. But these losses were easily replaced. The Luftwaffe lost 280 aeroplanes and more than 200 airmen killed, wounded or captured. Of the 70 Germans pilots who attacked B-61 alone, 29 were shot down and four aircraft were damaged.

For the Luftwaffe, Operation Bodenplatte was a staggering blow that accelerated the end of the Third Reich.

A Luftwaffe Focke Wulf Fw-190 fighter breaks up in mid-air under the guns of an Allied fighter during Operation Bodenplatte. (US Air Force via Wikimedia Commons)

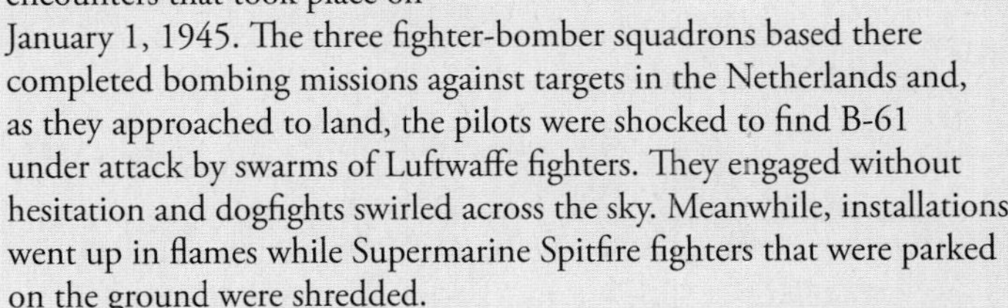

American Republic P-47 Thunderbolt fighter-bombers, caught on the ground during Operation Bodenplatte, lie destroyed at airfield Y-34 in France. (US Air Force via Wikimedia Commons)

American soldiers take cover against incoming Japanese fire near Baguio, Luzon, during the 1945 liberation of the Philippines. (US Army via Wikimedia Commons)

AMERICAN FORCES LAND ON LUZON

As the liberation of the Philippines from the Japanese entered a new phase, troops of the US Sixth Army, more than 175,000-strong, stormed ashore on the main island of Luzon. The landings took place at Lingayen Gulf on the northwestern coast of the island, and the main objective of the continuing offensive was two-fold: the elimination of the defending Japanese garrison and the liberation of the capital city of Manila, the 'Pearl of the Orient'.

In dramatic fashion, General Douglas MacArthur, commander of Allied forces in the Southwest Pacific, had made good on his pledge to return to the Philippines, wading ashore at Leyte in October 1944 and beseeching the Filipino people to rally with him in defeating the Japanese, who had controlled the islands since their tremendous victory in the spring of 1942. After an arduous six-week campaign, Leyte had been declared secure on Christmas Day 1944, and the might of the Sixth Army, under General Walter Kreuger, shifted northward.

The Americans encountered little resistance on the ground during the early stages of the Lingayen landings, although Japanese air attacks harassed the naval support contingent, sinking the escort carrier *Ommaney Bay* and four other ships while damaging 47 others in suicide Kamikaze attacks between January 3 and 13. However, despite the absence of immediate concerted resistance on land, the Japanese were determined to fight.

To that end, General Tomoyuki Yamashita, the 'Tiger of Malaya' whose lightning conquests of 1942 had astounded the world, was called on to lead the defence of Philippines. With 275,000 troops at his disposal, Yamashita was under no illusions that the Americans would strike hard on Luzon and move as rapidly as possible to wrest control of Manila from the Japanese. Without substantial air or naval support, Yamashita realised that his best tactic was to oppose the Americans in the field for as long as possible, taking a heavy toll in casualties and maintaining the forlorn hope that some cease-fire arrangement might be reached that would allow Japan to retain at least partial control of the Philippines.

US aircraft pounded the vicinity of the Luzon landings, and warships of the Third Fleet under Admiral William F 'Bull' Halsey added pre-invasion bombardment to the American muscle that came ashore at Lingayen Gulf. Yamashita understood that holding the beaches would be an exercise in futility and chose to oppose the Sixth Army with three distinctive defensive forces. In the mountains east of Manila, the 80,000 troops of the Shimbu Group were dug in and waiting, while the Kembu Group, numbering

General Douglas MacArthur pushed for a rapid advance in the liberation of Luzon and ultimately Manila. (US Army via Wikimedia Commons)

The first wave of American soldiers churns towards the shores of Luzon at Lingayen Gulf, January 1945. (US Government via Wikimedia Commons)

American and Japanese troops clash amid the dense jungle of Luzon in the spring of 1945. (US Army Center of Military History via Wikimedia Commons)

Soldiers of the US 129th Infantry Regiment call in artillery support against Japanese positions near Bayambang, Luzon. (US Department of Defense via Wikimedia Commons)

30,000, was ordered to occupy hills about 40 miles north of the capital and prevent the Americans from seizing the former US Army Air Forces base at Clark Field. Yamashita further took personal command of the Shobu Group, which included all the rather meagre number of tanks and vehicles the defenders could muster, intending to harass Krueger's drive to the south with 152,000 soldiers poised in the rugged country of northeastern Luzon.

Gen MacArthur had hoped to take Manila and stage a large victory parade to coincide with his 65th birthday on January 26, 1945. However, such aspirations were quickly dashed. Krueger was required to protect his flanks during the thrust toward Manila and dispatched two full divisions to take on Yamashita's Shobu Group while other units fought against the entrenched positions of the Kembu Group. Control of roads and railways that led to Manila was a priority, and the enemy contested the advance at every advantageous point.

MacArthur became dissatisfied with the progress of the Sixth Army, not only due to time constraints, but also because of the increasing probability that the Japanese would defend Manila rather than abandon the beautiful city as Yamashita had initially proposed. Further, he was well aware of the plight of thousands of American military and civilian personnel held amid squalid conditions in Japanese prison camps around the city for nearly three years.

As the campaign progressed, the US Eighth Army, under General Robert Eichelberger, moved from Leyte to Luzon on January 29, splashing ashore between San Narciso and San Antonio on the west coast of the island. The Eighth Army was tasked with clearing the Japanese from southern Luzon and then turning to join the Sixth Army in a pincer movement against Yamashita. Two days later, the 11th Airborne Division, under the command of General Joseph Swing, came ashore from landing craft at the beaches around Nasugbu, approximately 30 miles southwest of the former US naval base at Cavite, a few miles south of Manila. Altogether, these movements constituted a concerted effort to surround and then occupy the capital.

Within weeks, American forces had secured most of their strategic and tactical objectives on Luzon. However, the Japanese did indeed refuse to evacuate Manila. A costly fight for the city began in early February, and the city was devastated before it was secured on March 4.

The Luzon campaign resulted in the highest net casualty rate among US forces in World War Two with more than 8,000 killed, 32,000 wounded and almost 87,000 incapacitated due to disease and other non-combat related circumstances. The fighting resulted in nearly 193,000 Japanese killed and more than 9,500 taken prisoner.

Pockets of organised Japanese resistance held out on Luzon and elsewhere in the Philippines until hostilities ceased on August 15, 1945, and World War Two in the Pacific ended.

Soldiers of the 11th Airborne Division march through a Filipino village on January 31, 1945. (US Army Signal Corps via Wikimedia Commons)

RED ARMY LAUNCHES VISTULA-ODER OFFENSIVE

Above left: Soviet self-propelled assault guns and trucks enter the city of Lodz, Poland, during the Vistula-Oder Offensive. (Government of Ukraine via Wikimedia Commons)

Above right: Marshal Georgi Zhukov led the stunning advance of the Red Army 1st Belorussian Front during the Vistula-Oder Offensive. (US Government via Wikimedia Commons)

Taking advantage of its bridgehead across the River Vistula near Sandomierz in southern Poland, the Soviet Red Army unleashed its Vistula-Oder offensive, which would eventually make substantial gains, pushing the Germans 300 miles eastward from the River Vistula to the banks of the River Oder just over 40 miles from Berlin itself, in roughly five weeks of fighting.

The first Soviet troops committed were those of the 1st Ukrainian Front, under Marshal Ivan Konev. Two days later, on January 14, the 1st Belorussian Front, under Marshal Georgi Zhukov, and the 2nd Belorussian Front, under Marshal Konstantin Rokossovsky, plunged across bridgeheads closer to the Polish capital of Warsaw. In concert, these thrusts tore a gaping 200 mile wide hole in the German front.

By late December 1944, worrisome intelligence reports had filtered into the German high command. The reports indicated that 225 Red Army divisions were poised to strike at the German line, which had been depleted due to Soviet pressure further south through the Balkans, Hungary and Yugoslavia. German Chief of Staff General Heinz Guderian warned that his 50 depleted infantry and 12 weary panzer divisions would be insufficient to stem the Soviet tide, but Hitler demurred, refusing to halt the Ardennes offensive in the West and transfer reinforcements to meet this potentially lethal threat.

Within five days, Zhukov's troops had taken Warsaw, while the tip of Konev's armoured spear had penetrated to the frontier of Silesia on the doorstep of the Third Reich. The astonishing rapidity of the Soviet onslaught, swiftly covering 100 miles of territory across a front that had expanded to 400 miles wide, staggered the Germans. Hitler's ineptitude and lack of tactical understanding became glaringly apparent when he finally halted the western offensive, but chose to send reinforcements, primarily the Sixth Panzer Army, into Hungary to defend Budapest rather than into Poland where the defenders were critically overmatched.

Therefore, for two more weeks, the Soviet rampage through Poland continued. In the centre, Zhukov struck from Warsaw all the way to Pomerania and the old Prussian province of Brandenburg. Meanwhile, Konev bridged the Oder near Breslau and severed critical supply lines

from Germany. In another heavy blow, Rokossovsky roared all the way to the Gulf of Danzig and cut off 25 German divisions in East Prussia.

Hitler's next foolhardy move had been to appoint Reichsführer Heinrich Himmler to command the newly-formed Army Group Vistula with orders to halt the Soviets. Himmler had no military experience and surrounded himself with equally unsuited SS cronies.

At the end of January, Zhukov paused on the lower Oder at Küstrin about 40 miles from Berlin. Konev continued through Sommerfeld and the River Neisse, fewer than 80 miles from the Nazi capital, by February 15. More bloody fighting lay ahead, but the stage was set for the epic Battle of Berlin.

Under a white flag, German officers walk towards negotiations with the Soviets to surrender the city of Breslau. (Government of Poland via Wikimedia Commons)

BRITISH FORCES CLEAR ROER TRIANGLE

A British soldier fires at German positions north of the Dutch town of Sittard during Operation Blackcock. (Collections of the Imperial War Museums via Wikimedia Commons)

In a prerequisite to the major Allied offensive into the German Rhineland, the British Second Army launched Operation Blackcock, an effort to clear enemy forces from defensive positions in the so-called 'Roer Triangle'.

Geographically, the Roer Triangle was bounded by the town of Heinsberg in Germany and the villages of Roermond and Sittard in the Netherlands. Crossings of the Rivers Maas, Roer and Wurm would facilitate the destruction of elements of the German 15th Army in the area, including the two infantry divisions, the 176th and 183rd, of the XII SS Panzer Corps, positioned between the towns of Roermond and Geilenkirchen, and Fallschirmjäger Regiment Hübner, commanded by Lieutenant Colonel Friedrich Hübner, positioned on the northern flank of the SS formations under the command of General Günther Blumentritt.

The British Second Army committed General Neil Ritchie's XII Corps, including the famed 7th Armoured Division's Desert Rats, the 43rd Wessex Infantry Division and the 52nd Lowland Infantry Division to the attack. If successful, the British front would be extended further into Germany and provide staging areas for the subsequent advance into the Rhineland.

British forces attacked on three axes, the 7th Armoured taking the bridge across the Roer at Sint Odiliënberg on the left, the 52nd Lowland Division capturing Heinsberg in the centre, and the 43rd Wessex Division advancing southeast of Dremmen to exploit the breach in the German perimeter created by the 52nd Lowland Division.

Each objective was accomplished in two weeks of fighting that concluded on January 27, 1945. Casualties were moderate to heavy, and the decisive engagement of Blackcock occurred at the Dutch town of Sint Joost, where combat raged for four days with the airborne troops of

Fallschirmjäger Regiment Hübner contesting the northward advance of 7th Armoured towards Montfort, another town in the Netherlands. Approximately two companies of German soldiers occupied Sint Joost, and they fought tenaciously, repelling three heavy assaults by the Desert Rats before the fighting subsided. The Germans suffered more than 100 killed and many wounded, while the British sustained 77 casualties from the Rifle Brigade and the Durham Light Infantry.

After giving up Sint Joost, the Germans were compelled to retire from the Roer Triangle. Their losses included roughly 2,000 killed, wounded and captured. British casualties totalled 1,152. During Operation Blackcock, Hawker Typhoon fighter-bombers of the Royal Canadian Air Force's No. 143 Wing conducted multiple raids on Montfort, damaging virtually every building in the town and resulting in scores of civilian casualties.

On February 8, the First Canadian Army initiated the campaign into the Rhineland with Operation Veritable to the north while the US Ninth Army launched Operation Grenade in the south two weeks later in a major pincer movement.

Above: In whitewash camouflage, a British Cromwell tank of the 7th Armoured Division rolls through a street in a Dutch town on January 16, 1945. (Collections of the Imperial War Museums via Wikimedia Commons)

Below: Captured at the German frontier village of Hongen, Wehrmacht soldiers trudge towards the rear during Operation Blackcock. (Collections of the Imperial War Museums via Wikimedia Commons)

RED ARMY ENTERS WARSAW

Five days after the initiation of its Vistula-Oder Offensive, the Red Army entered the war-ravaged Polish capital city of Warsaw. Soldiers of the First Belorussian Front and the First Ukrainian Front, under Marshals Georgi Zhukov and Ivan Konev, moved into Warsaw as the previously occupying Nazis pulled back to avoid encirclement. The advance occurred nearly six months after the Red Army had halted outside Warsaw during the uprising of the Polish Home Army, intended to eject the Nazis and facilitate the liberation of the city.

As the Red Army initially approached the Polish capital in late July 1944, Soviet Premier Josef Stalin encouraged the Home Army to launch its revolt against the occupying Nazis. In turn, the Warsaw Uprising was ignited on August 1 as roughly 50,000 Polish freedom fighters took up arms. However, the expectation of the Poles that Soviet arms, equipment, food and supplies were forthcoming, was dashed in the midst of the street fighting.

Stalin, a ruthless and pragmatic practitioner of 'realpolitik', reneged on his promise and ordered the Red Army to halt short of Warsaw. In practice, the Soviet leader allowed the Germans to fight the uprising without interference, eliminating the majority of forces that were perceived loyal to the Polish government in exile in London. Thereby, the Soviet government enabled a pro-Soviet regime to assert control in Poland while the Red Army had swept across much of the country and backed Stalin's political play with real military might.

Fighters of the Polish Home Army battle the Nazis during the Warsaw Uprising of 1944. (Republic of Poland via Wikimedia Commons)

Despite long odds and the consternation at Stalin's inaction, the Home Army gained control of much of Warsaw during three days of bitter fighting, but was unable to take control of critical transportation and communication centres. In turn, the Germans launched a brutal counterattack in August and massacred approximately 40,000 Polish civilians. Rather than a rapid revolt soon supported by troops and tanks of the Red Army, the Warsaw Uprising devolved into a lengthy siege-like operation. The Germans methodically rooted fighting Poles out of houses, entrenchments and barricades, meting out summary executions and laying waste to even more of the beleaguered city. The uprising was effectively ended with the surrender of the Home Army on October 2, 1944.

By that time, even Stalin had been compelled to provide limited humanitarian aid, although he had prevented the Western Allies from intervening across a significant distance for several months.

When the Red Army entered Warsaw, among its ranks were the soldiers of the First Polish Army, crossing into the city through the ruins along the left bank of the River Vistula. Only weak German resistance was encountered – thanks in no small measure to the sacrifice of the Home Army, which inflicted approximately 16,000 casualties on the Nazis.

Carrying infantrymen atop their hulls, tanks of the Soviet Red Army roll forward during the Vistula-Oder Offensive. (Government of Ukraine via Wikimedia Commons)

Soldiers of the First Polish Army stand in a devastated Warsaw street after the city's 1945 liberation from the Nazis. (Republic of Poland via Wikimedia Commons)

RED ARMY LIBERATES AUSCHWITZ

German officers and guards separate arriving Jews into groups at the Auschwitz rail line in the spring of 1944. (US Government via Wikimedia Commons)

Steadily pushing the German 371st and 359th Infantry Divisions back from their defensive positions around the town of Oswiecim in southern Poland, four rifle divisions of the Soviet Red Army, the 100th, 107th, 286th and 322nd, came across a complex of labour and extermination areas known to the Nazis as Auschwitz.

The sprawling Auschwitz death camps, liberated two weeks after the initiation of the Red Army Vistula-Oder Offensive, revealed the appalling extent of the Nazis brutality during their campaign of extermination against European Jewry and other "undesirable" ethnic groups including homosexuals, Jehovah's Witnesses, communists and political opponents and gypsies. The first mass transportation of Jews to Auschwitz, which had originally served as a troop barracks and then a prisoner of war camp, occurred on March 25, 1942, and during the next four-and-a-half years murders were committed on an incredible scale.

During his war crimes trial at Nuremberg, former Auschwitz commandant Rudolf Höss expressed great pride in the "full production" rate of 16,000 deaths per day among inmates, and an estimated 1.1 million people died in the Nazi death factory. In his memoirs, published after his execution by hanging in the grounds of the death camp, Höss wrote that through it all: "I was completely normal… even when I was carrying out the task of extermination I lived a normal life".

Prior to abandoning Auschwitz, the Germans had attempted to destroy as much of the complex as possible and evacuated many inmates westwards. However, about 9,000 starving and ill prisoners were still in the camp on the day of liberation. Actually, when the Red Army reached Auschwitz the discovery did not generate much interest. The concentration camp at Majdanek had been liberated the previous July as the Soviets captured the city of Lublin, so Red Army commanders and Soviet leaders were aware of the existence of Nazi atrocities. Western newspapers had published photos of Majdanek, but given the rapid pace of Allied forces during the last days of World War Two, there were other events to cover. The extent of the heinous crimes at Auschwitz, therefore, would not come sharply into focus for months.

The Red Army liberators reported their grisly discovery, but Marshal Ivan Konev, commander of the 1st Ukrainian Front, declined to tour the camp. He said: "It was not that I did not want to see that death camp with my own eyes," he later wrote. "I simply made up my mind not to see it. The combat operations were in full swing, and to command them was such a strain that I could find neither time nor justification for abandoning myself to my emotions. During the war I did not belong to myself."

On July 2, 1947, the Polish government established a state memorial on the Auschwitz site.

Convicted war criminal and former Auschwitz commandant Rudolf Höss is led to the gallows in 1947. (Government of Poland via Wikimedia Commons)

In this still from a Soviet film on the liberation of Auschwitz, children who have survived the ordeal of the concentration camp gaze at their Red Army liberators. (United States Holocaust Memorial Museum, courtesy of Belarussian State Archive of Documentary Film and Photography via Wikimedia Commons)

BATTLE OF MANILA BEGINS

Nearly a month after landings at Lingayen Gulf and other locations initiated the fight for the Philippine island of Luzon, US forces began the battle for control of the capital city of Manila. Renowned for its beauty and known as the 'Pearl of the Orient', the city was utterly destroyed in a month of armed convulsion that finally ended on March 3, 1945.

Japanese General Tomoyuki Yamashita, tasked with defending the Philippines against their would-be liberators, understood the monumental task before him and chose to fight a battle of attrition on Luzon. Yamashita had hoped that all Japanese forces would abandon Manila and co-operate in the fighting across the rugged terrain of the island, exacting a heavy price in American casualties and buying time for the preparation of other defences of the Japanese home islands, which were threatened more and more with each passing day.

However, in the event, Yamashita did not control the contingent of Imperial Japanese Navy troops of the 31st Naval Special Base Force that garrisoned Manila, 12,500-strong under the command of Rear Admiral Sanji Iwabuchi. Determined to oppose the Americans to the last, Iwabuchi turned the fanatical defence of Manila into a spectacular exercise of death and destruction.

Filipino civilians run for their lives through a Manila street as Japanese troops approach in February 1945. (US Department of Defense via Wikimedia Commons)

the Nips, bounce off the Nips, save your men, but get to Manila! Free the internees at Santo Tomas. Take the Malacanang Palace and the Legislative Building."

The battle for Manila was marked by several sharp encounters. The campus of Santo Tomas University had been converted to a prisoner of war camp, where many American and Filipino prisoners had languished for more than three years. Santo Tomas was cleared on February 5 after a stand-off with the Japanese, who held some prisoners hostage in the university's education building. A day earlier, more than 1,000 prisoners had been freed from Bilibid Prison in the city.

On February 6, MacArthur prematurely announced that Manila had fallen. Weeks of fighting remained, and a nexus of resistance was the walled fortress of the Intramuros, where numerous stately buildings held government offices. The battle for the Intramuros began on February 23, and American tanks and artillery were forced to bombard the area heavily to dislodge the defenders. The urban combat experienced was perhaps the most intense of World War Two.

When the Battle of Manila ended, along with the destruction of the city the Americans lost more than 1,000 dead and nearly 5,600 wounded. Japanese casualties were substantially higher with at least 16,000 killed, most of these in the fight for the Intramuros.

American soldiers advance through the ruins of a building in Manila. Much of the fighting in the Philippine capital was house-to-house and street-to-street. (National Archives and Records Administration via Wikimedia Commons)

Meanwhile, General Douglas MacArthur, supreme Allied commander in the Southwest Pacific, was growing restless and prodded General Walter Kreuger, commander of the Sixth Army, to strike toward the capital swiftly. Long ties to the Philippines tugged at MacArthur's heartstrings, as did a desire to liberate Manila with a great parade that coincided with his upcoming 65th birthday. However, the general's plan was thwarted in the swirl of combat that destroyed the Pearl of the Orient and left at least 100,000 Filipino civilians dead, most of them victims of Japanese atrocities.

The American drive to Manila developed as a large pincer movement with the Sixth Army bearing down from the north while General Robert Eichelberger's Eighth Army advanced from the south after moving to Luzon following the end of the fighting on nearby Leyte. The 11th Airborne Division also participated in the advance.

On January 31, MacArthur barked to General Vernon D Mudge, commander of the 1st Cavalry Division: "Go to Manila! Go around

The once beautiful city of Manila, the 'Pearl of the Orient', was utterly destroyed during its liberation in early 1945. (US Army via Wikimedia Commons)

ALLIED BOMBS KILL JUDGE FREISLER

Odious Judge Roland Freisler, a zealous Nazi, was killed by Allied bombs during an air raid on the German capital of Berlin. US Army Air Forces Boeing B-17 Flying Fortresses of the Eighth Air Force, based in England, struck numerous administrative buildings in the city and disrupted the proceedings in Freisler's courtroom.

A veteran of the German Army in World War One and a former prisoner of war, Freisler officially had served as State Secretary of the Reich Ministry of Justice and presided as President of the People's Court from 1942 until his death. Appointed to various judicial positions in prior years, he contributed to the Nazification of German law. One of the framers of the 'Final Solution to the Jewish Question' that set the Holocaust in motion, Freisler attended the infamous Wannsee Conference held on the outskirts of Berlin in 1942 during which plans were made to effect the extermination of European Jewry.

In this 1942 photo, Judge Roland Freisler stands (left) while conferring with other Nazi legal theorists. (Creative Commons Bundesarchiv Bild via Wikimedia Commons)

During the years of World War Two, Roland Freisler presided over several of the most notorious prosecutions of the Nazi era. The proceedings of his kangaroo court typically involved hostile questioning of the accused punctuated with boisterous harangues against enemies of the Third Reich. He occupied the bench in Munich during the sham trials of Hans and Sophie Scholl, brother and sister members of the secret White Rose resistance movement. The two were sentenced to death and executed by guillotine on February 22, 1943. The guillotine was chosen as the method of execution rather than public hanging to avoid making anti-Nazi martyrs of the condemned. Freisler also presided over a second trial in which three White Rose defendants were sentenced to death, nine were given lengthy prison terms and one was acquitted.

While cameras recorded the proceedings, Freisler railed against accused conspirators in the July 20, 1944, plot to assassinate Adolf Hitler, particularly former Field Marshal Erwin von Witzleben, who stood before the judge in old, shabby and ill-fitting clothes he had been forced to wear.

After Freisler convened his court on the morning of February 3, 1945, the proceedings were disrupted by the American bombers. Just after 11am, the judge adjourned the People's Court and ordered the prisoners on trial to be taken to an air raid shelter. However, he lingered to gather papers concerning the upcoming disposition of the case of suspected July 20 conspirator Fabian von Schlabrendorff. It is believed that moments after clearing the courtroom, a bomb struck the building causing a heavy column to collapse on Freisler. He was crushed to death, the corpse further flattened when more debris fell. An alternative version of his death states that he was killed by a bomb fragment and died on the pavement outside the court building.

Regardless, Freisler's death was not mourned. He was buried in the cemetery of his wife's family. His name is not inscribed on the monument.

Left: An ardent Nazi, Judge Roland Freisler was killed when Allied bombers destroyed his courtroom. (Creative Commons Bundesarchiv Bild via Wikimedia Commons)

Right: With a bust of Hitler behind him, Judge Freisler convenes his Nazi kangaroo court. (Creative Commons Bundesarchiv Bild via Wikimedia Commons)

YALTA CONFERENCE BEGINS

The 'Big Three' appear before the press in an outwardly relaxed atmosphere during the Yalta Conference. (US Government via Wikimedia Commons)

At the resort town of Yalta in the Crimea, the Big Three – US President Franklin D Roosevelt (FDR), British Prime Minister Winston Churchill and Soviet Premier Josef Stalin – began a week-long series of meetings (concluding February 11), their second of three major summits conducted during the World War Two years.

Among the immediate topics for discussion were more detailed agreements for the government, reparations responsibilities and disposition of post-war Germany, the prospects for Soviet entry into the war against Japan, the formalisation of some aspects regarding the inception of the United Nations and the future of eastern European countries vis-à-vis spheres of influence.

The three leaders had previously affirmed that with the Nazi surrender, Germany would be divided into four occupation zones under the administration of the United States, Great Britain, the Soviet Union and France. Although the millions of displaced civilian refugees and repatriated Wehrmacht POWs would be facing incredible hardship amid the devastation of their country, the leaders agreed that only minimal aid would be extended to avert rampant starvation and disease. They agreed that Germany would undergo a systematic programme of de-Nazification involving the removal of all public images related to the defeated regime, dismantling of the Nazi governmental apparatus and a purge of former Nazi leaders to include arrest, incarceration, trial, sentencing and carrying out of verdicts. This decision was later set in motion with the trials of 24 top Nazis accused of war crimes during the tribunal at Nuremberg that was set to begin in November 1945.

Further, German industry was to be rendered incapable of producing weapons of war or supporting a military in the waging of waging offensive war. The question of reparations, which had been a cornerstone of the Treaty of Versailles in 1919, was handed over to a commission for in-depth study.

In the spring of 1945, the Soviet Red Army was at the height of its power. The Soviet Union had sustained grievous losses, both military and civilian, during nearly four years of fighting against the Nazis. Bearing the brunt of the battle, the Soviets sustained an estimated 20 million dead, but the Red Army had steadily pushed westwards and now occupied much of eastern Europe. Amid discussions surrounding the future

governments of countries such as Poland, Czechoslovakia, Hungary, Romania and Bulgaria, Roosevelt and Churchill were compelled to recognise that these nations were already under Soviet influence.

Just months before assuming the post of US Secretary of State, James F Byrnes served as a delegate at Yalta. He wrote later: "It was not a question of what we would let the Russians do, but what we could get the Russians to do." In the event, negotiations concluded with the Soviets agreeing to free elections in the occupied countries. However, Poland was a prime example of the real widening ideological gap between East and West. Great Britain and the US supported the government in exile based in London, while the Soviets were backing the Polish Committee of National Liberation, dominated by communists and based in Lublin.

Given the circumstances, Stalin's pledge of free elections was the best the Western Allies could hope for. The Soviet sphere of influence was solidifying, and the seeds of the Cold War were being sown. In the end, the Soviet leader failed to keep his promise of free elections and Churchill later lamented that the cloak of an "Iron Curtain" descended across eastern Europe.

Members of the US delegation to the Yalta Conference gather. Among those pictured are President Roosevelt, Army Chief of Staff General George C Marshall, Chief of Naval Operations Fleet Admiral Ernest J King, and Secretary of State Edward Stettinius. (US Government via Wikimedia Commons)

Members of the Soviet, British and US delegations gather informally at the Yalta Conference. (Creative Commons Ministry of Defence of the Russian Federation via Wikimedia Commons)

seats in the General Assembly. The formalisation of Security Council procedures included the establishment of five permanent seats – the US, Britain, Soviet Union, China and France – each with veto power regarding decisions made by this controlling body.

The Yalta Conference is seen by both critics and advocates as a watershed in the history of the post-World War Two era. During the meetings, Roosevelt's health was visibly failing and within two months of their conclusion, he would be dead of a cerebral haemorrhage. Some historians have questioned his abilities to negotiate effectively and assert that the US and Great Britain sold out eastern Europe to a half-century of Cold War communist repression. At the same time, Churchill was confronted with the reality that with or without his old friend FDR the United States and the Soviet Union would emerge from the global conflict as the two dominant superpowers on the world stage.

British Prime Minister Winston Churchill sits (right) during the Yalta negotiations. Soviet Premier Josef Stalin is on the left and US President Roosevelt far right. (Creative Commons Ministry of Defence of the Russian Federation via Wikimedia Commons)

As for the question of Soviet participation in the war against Japan, Stalin agreed to declare war within three months of the defeat of Nazi Germany. At the time of the Yalta Conference, both Churchill and Roosevelt considered Soviet military involvement critical in the anticipated fighting on the Asian continent. However, this issue was rendered moot with the US atomic bombs dropped on Hiroshima and Nagasaki five months later.

At least in the interim, Stalin was promised a wide sphere of influence in Asia. The territories lost to Japan in the 1904-1905 Russo-Japanese War were to be recovered, while Soviet domination would extend even further, including the continuation of a pro-communist government in Outer Mongolia, further influence in Manchuria with its vital railroads and Soviet possession of the Kuril Islands and the southern half of Sakhalin Island. Stalin also agreed to sign a pact of friendship with the government of China, a vast country soon to resume its civil war following the defeat of Japan.

Furthering their agreements regarding the United Nations, Stalin did drop his demand that all 16 Soviet Socialist Republics should have

Top: President Roosevelt's frailty is evident in this photo taken during the Yalta Conference proceedings. (Government of the United Kingdom via Wikimedia Commons)

Right: Prime Minister Winston Churchill prepares to light a cigar as Soviet Premier Josef Stalin (left) beams, during the Yalta Conference. (US Army Signal Corps via Wikimedia Commons)

FRENCH FORCES ELIMINATE COLMAR POCKET

French forces eliminated the Colmar Pocket, inflicting casualties, taking prisoners and compelling the Germans to relinquish their last piece of French territory. The long-disputed provinces of Alsace and Lorraine had changed hands historically between Germany and France. During World War Two, the Nazis occupied the area and, following the Allied landings in Normandy on June 6, 1944, and in southern France on August 15 of that year, the decisive battle for control of the provinces concluded soon after the final defeat of Hitler's Ardennes Offensive to the north.

In November 1944, the Allies had succeeded in advancing to the River Rhine in the south, obliging German forces to retreat across the natural barrier. However, operations intended to clear Alsace of enemy forces were temporarily stalled as the US Sixth Army Group successfully cleared northern and southern Alsace, but stopped short of ejecting the Germans from the central area of the province.

The remaining German presence on the west bank of the Rhine was centred on the town of Colmar and consisted of roughly 850sq miles of territory. The German 19th Army, commanded by General Siegfried Rasp, consisted of General Max Grimmeiss' LXIV Corps and General Erich Abraham's LXIII Corps, a total of seven under-strength divisions available to oppose the decisive Allied push to occupy the entirety of Alsace.

By early February, the French First Army, under General Jean de Lattre de Tassigny, supported by troops and tanks of the US XXI

Second Lieutenant Audie Murphy, a hero of the fighting in the Colmar Pocket, shown in uniform with many of his decorations. He later became a film actor. (US Army via Wikimedia Commons)

Army Corps, had successfully driven the Nazis completely out of France. Sixth Army Group commander General Jacob Devers allotted the French 2nd Armored Division and the US 28th Infantry Division to bolster the effort and anticipated transferring more reinforcements as they became available.

Gen de Tassigny formulated a plan of double envelopment to reduce the Colmar Pocket and began his attacks in late January. After a 30-minute artillery bombardment, the four divisions of General Emile Bethouart's French I Corps advanced in the south on January 20, intending to divert German attention and draw off reserves. On the 22nd, the French II Corps, under General Joseph de Goislard de Monsabert, advanced on the flank of the US 3rd Infantry Division as heavy snow and foul winter weather abated. Among the heroes in the heavy fighting was 2nd Lieutenant Audie Murphy, the most decorated soldier in American military history, who earned the Medal of Honor on January 26 while commanding an infantry company of the 15th Regiment.

Progress was slow at times, particularly in the French I Corps sector where the Germans tenaciously defended the town of Riedwihr, but in 20 days of combat the enemy was finally forced completely out of France and the Allies followed up, poised to cross the Rhine into the Fatherland itself. The cost of victory included 13,000 French casualties, 8,000 Americans killed, wounded or captured, and 25,000 German soldiers lost.

American and French Moroccan soldiers greet one another in the town of Rouffach, France, during the reduction of the Colmar Pocket. (US Army via Wikimedia Commons)

A light tank of the US 12th Armored Division keeps watch in the town square of Rouffach, France. (National Archives and Records Administration via Wikimedia Commons)

German defenders fire a mortar at oncoming American troops during the Battle of Hürtgen Forest.
(Creative Commons Bundesarchiv Bild via Wikimedia Commons)

A US Army half-track grinds its way along a muddy road during the fighting in the Hürtgen Forest, early 1945.
(US Army via Wikimedia Commons)

BATTLE OF HÜRTGEN FOREST ENDS

The Battle of Hürtgen Forest, longest in the history of the US Army, ended after the Americans pulled out of the expansive killing zone that had drained them of lives and resources since September 1944.

Begun with the intent to breach the German Siegfried Line (or Westwall) defences, secure bridgeheads across the natural barrier of the River Rhine, and strike deep into the territory of the Third Reich, the offensive into the Hürtgen was undertaken by US First Army commander General Courtney Hodges, who assessed the tactical situation as American soldiers were engaged with the enemy for control of the city of Aachen, the seat of Charlemagne's Holy Roman Empire. Aachen would soon become the first German city to fall into American hands.

While the fighting in the city was under way, Hodges and his subordinate General J Lawton Collins, commanding the US VII Corps, decided to continue their advance south and east of Aachen. Their reasoning appeared sound at first cut. However, the Hürtgen was a densely wooded area of roughly 50sq miles, hardly good tank country and difficult for infantry manoeuvre due to the rugged terrain. Rather than bypass the Hürtgen, Hodges and Collins decided to clear enemy forces from the area while also protecting the flank of VII Corps. Although no immediate effort would be made to seize the seven dams that controlled the flow of water into the surrounding valley from the River Roer and its tributaries, this would soon become a priority.

The Germans had not expected an Allied thrust into the grim woods of the Hürtgen, but nevertheless fortified the area with pillboxes, bunkers and machine gun nests. Minefields were sown, while elements of the veteran Seventh, Fifteenth and Fifth Panzer Armies were committed to man these stout defensive positions. Not long after the first probing attacks into the forest, the Americans ran into vigorous German resistance and the battle devolved into a bloody stalemate – attrition at its worst.

Historians continue to debate the wisdom of the advance into the Hürtgen Forest, considering that the early objective was merely to cover the flank of VII Corps with little relevance assigned to the flood control associated with the Roer dams. An advance to the southeast would

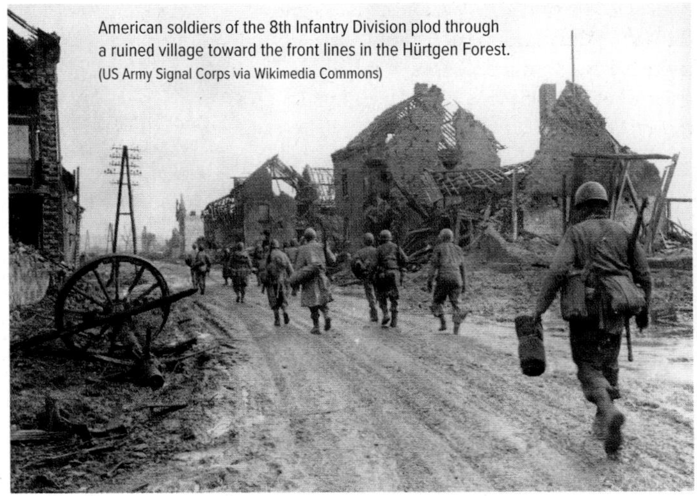
American soldiers of the 8th Infantry Division plod through a ruined village toward the front lines in the Hürtgen Forest.
(US Army Signal Corps via Wikimedia Commons)

probably have facilitated the seizure of these dams, from which the Germans could unleash a torrent of water that would stop Allied advances in the region immediately, while avoiding the tangle of the forest.

In actuality, the Americans hammered away at the Hürtgen defences, eventually committing elements of the 9th, 28th, 1st, 8th, 78th and 83rd Infantry Divisions to the meatgrinder along with the 3rd and 5th Armored Divisions, the 517th Parachute Infantry Regiment and the 2nd Ranger Battalion. US soldiers were tested beyond belief, enduring the persistent German fire and the harsh winter weather conditions.

Only with the onset of the German Ardennes Offensive in December 1944 did the US begin pulling out of the Hürtgen Forest. The losses had been staggering – 33,000 killed, wounded, captured or removed from the combat zone due to other causes such as frostbite and illness. Many veterans of the terrible battle suffered post-traumatic stress disorder (PTSD) and were unable to return to duty after days in the line in the dismal forest. German casualties were estimated at 28,000.

BOMBING OF DRESDEN

Led by nine swift de Havilland Mosquito pathfinders to identify the target with incendiaries, 796 Avro Lancaster heavy bombers of the Royal Air Force droned above the German city of Dresden, capital of the province of Saxony, and unleashed a torrent of nocturnal destruction.

Until this fateful night, Dresden, unlike many other major cities of the Third Reich, had been virtually unscathed. However, the devil came to exact his due. The RAF bombs ignited a conflagration like no other, save perhaps that experienced in Hamburg in 1943. High winds whipped the flames into a veritable firestorm that consumed oxygen, buildings and people. Some citizens were simply smothered as the air supply in bomb shelters evaporated. Others were incinerated where they stood. Still others fled into the waters of the River Elbe to escape the stifling heat.

The following day, Boeing B-17 Flying Fortress bombers of the US Eighth Air Force bombed Dresden yet again, guided this time to their target by the massive pall of smoke punctuated with tongues of flame that hovered over the city. They came again on March 2, 1945, and when the Allied bombers had wrought their destruction, an estimated 30,000 to 60,000 people, the vast majority of them civilians, had died.

The devastating raids occurred just three months prior to the end of World War Two in Europe, and a 1953 US bomb damage assessment revealed the extent of the devastation – roughly 23% of Dresden's industrial buildings and 50% of its residential structures destroyed or heavily damaged. RAF bomb damage reports concluded that 78,000 residential structures were completely destroyed and another 27,700 rendered unliveable. The human cost created another dimension of a searing debate that continues today.

The bombing of Dresden remains one of the most controversial episodes of World War Two. With the Allies so close to victory, had the devastation been necessary? Was the raid, in fact, a war crime, particularly because of the heavy toll in civilian casualties? Considering these questions, the context of the time is relevant. Earlier in the war, the British people had suffered mightily as their cities were relentlessly pounded during the Luftwaffe Blitz of 1940-1941.

Retribution, therefore, was 'devoutly to be wished'. The catalyst for such retaliation was personified by Marshal of the Royal Air Force Sir Arthur 'Bomber' Harris, appointed chief of RAF Bomber Command in February 1942. Harris reasoned that the German ability to wage war lay not only in its military capabilities, but in the source of those capabilities and their sustenance – the German industrial base and

Gutted and blackened buildings are visible for miles in this post-February 1945 image taken from the Dresden city hall. (Deutsche Fotothek via Wikimedia Commons)

A statue of Martin Luther stands starkly against a backdrop of destroyed buildings in Dresden. (Creative Commons Bundesarchiv Bild via Wikimedia Commons)

A superb weapon of war, the Avro Lancaster heavy bomber delivered destruction during raids on German cities. (Open Government License Cpl Phil Major ABIPP via Wikimedia Commons)

Left: Marshal of the Royal Air Force Sir Arthur 'Bomber' Harris was the architect of the RAF bombing offensive. (Collections of the Imperial War Museums via Wikimedia Commons)

Above: The extent of the destruction wrought in Dresden is starkly visible in this 1945 photo. (Creative Commons Bundesarchiv Bild via Wikimedia Commons)

This view of Old Town Dresden taken in 1910 conveys a sense of the city's picturesque beauty. (Public Domain Unknown Author via Wikimedia Commons)

the people who worked in the factories that produced munitions. Total war meant war against the civilian population, and eventually a campaign of sustained round-the-clock bombing of German cities took shape, the RAF bombing at night and the Eighth Air Force by day, giving the devil no respite.

Harris warned of what was coming, swearing with a reference to the Old Testament book of Hosea: "They sowed the wind, and now they are going to reap the whirlwind." The early RAF raids were conducted with relatively few bombers, but the numbers grew steadily to the first 1,000-aeroplane raids in the spring of 1942. And soon the Americans joined in.

That summer, RAF aircraft delivered a chilling message to the German people, leaflets fluttering down with a warning. "We are bombing Germany, city by city, and ever more terribly, in order to make it impossible for you to go on with the war. That is our object. We shall pursue it remorselessly. City by city: Lübeck, Rostock, Cologne, Emden, Bremen, Wilhelmshaven, Duisburg, Hamburg – and the list will grow longer and longer. Let the Nazis drag you down to disaster with them if you will. That is for you to decide. We are coming by day and by night. No part of the Reich is safe. People who work in [factories] live close to them. Therefore, we hit your houses, and you."

Despite the fact that Dresden had been spared into 1945, it remained a potential target for military reasons as a centre of manufacturing, troop marshalling and transport and communications. By February, there were literally few major targets left in Germany. Questions surrounding the military necessity of the bombing emerged in the wake of the devastation, but Harris was resolute and responded forcefully: "No doubt in the past we were justified in attacking German cities," he declared. "But to do so was always repugnant and now that the Germans are beaten anyway we can properly abstain from proceeding with these attacks. This is a doctrine to which I could never subscribe. Attacks on cities like any other act of war are intolerable unless they are strategically justified. But they are strategically justified in so far as they tend to shorten the war and preserve the lives of Allied soldiers… I do not personally regard the whole of the remaining cities of Germany as worth the bones of one British Grenadier."

Strategic bombing was an instrument of total war, but the destruction of Dresden remains the subject of debate and conjecture. Even Prime Minister Winston Churchill considered the situation. After Dresden, he told Harris, bluntly: "It seems to me that the moment has come when the question of bombing German cities simply for the sake of increasing terror should be reviewed. Otherwise we shall come into control of an utterly ruined land." He further noted: "The destruction of Dresden remains a serious query against the conduct of Allied bombing."

In the post-war years, the raids on Dresden and Hamburg became symbols of strategic air power that shocked the civilised world. However, it must be stated that the suffering in Britain as the Luftwaffe had rained death on London, Coventry, Birmingham and other cities was at least its equal in brutality.

US MARINES LAND ON IWO JIMA

After prolonged bombardment of the island by sea and air, the first US Marines of the 4th and 5th Divisions, roughly 40,000-strong, churned towards the black sand beaches of Iwo Jima, in the Volcano Islands group.

Tasked with wresting control of the island – eight square miles of land shaped like a pork chop and only 750 miles from the Japanese capital of Tokyo – the Marines faced a determined enemy of approximately 25,000 defenders. The Battle for Iwo Jima stretched across 34 bloody days before the island was declared secure, and in the process 6,821 Marines were killed and 17,000 wounded. The Japanese garrison was virtually wiped out.

The rationale for the immense bloodshed at Iwo Jima was straightforward: The tenacity of the Japanese defence of numerous Pacific outposts as the Americans slogged their way along the island road to Tokyo had convinced US war planners that the ultimate victory would eventually require an actual invasion of the Japanese home islands and the occupation of Japan itself. Iwo Jima would provide an important staging area for further operations during the US island offensive.

Meanwhile, American Boeing B-29 Superfortress heavy bombers were already raining destruction on industrial targets in Japan. Flying from bases in the Mariana Islands, the B-29s were required to cover great distances on each mission. Crippled bombers and their precious crews were in great peril. However, three airstrips, two already completed and one under construction, could provide an emergency landing option for damaged bombers, saving aircraft and crews. Further, the capture of Iwo Jima would eliminate the use of the airstrips as bases for Japanese fighters.

The Marines expected a difficult fight for Iwo Jima, and General Tadamichi Kuribayashi, commanding the Japanese forces on the island, prepared formidable defences. Resigned to the eventual fate of his command, Kuribayashi committed to defence in depth and exhorted his men to give their lives for Emperor Hirohito. In doing so, he ordered them to take the lives of at least ten Americans, too.

Rather than confront the Marines on the beaches, Kuribayashi ordered the construction of an elaborate defensive network. The island was honeycombed with tunnels. Cave entrances were fortified. Machine-gun nests and artillery emplacements were positioned with interlocking fields of fire. Spider holes, large enough for only a single soldier, were dug into the volcanic terrain. The Japanese constructed pillboxes and bunkers that were reinforced with steel, concrete and heaps of sand to absorb the shockwaves of plunging naval fire. One Japanese observer noted that the Marines hit the beaches like a tidal

US Marines struggle ashore on the black sand beaches of Iwo Jima, February 19, 1945. (US Department of Defense via Wikimedia Commons)

With Mount Suribachi looming in the background, troops of the 1st Battalion, 23rd Marines take cover from Japanese fire on the beach at Iwo Jima. (US Department of Defense via Wikimedia Commons)

Troops of the 2nd Battalion, 27th Marines prepare to move inland while under Japanese fire at Iwo Jima. (US Navy via Wikimedia Commons)

was the island declared secure. The Marines took only 216 prisoners, and some 3,000 diehard enemy holdouts were still being rounded up or killed months later. Kuribayashi was reported to have died while leading one of the desperate Banzai charges or to have committed ritual suicide. His body was never found.

Even as fighting raged at Iwo Jima, its worth to the Americans was demonstrated. On the afternoon of March 4, 1945, the B-29 *Dinah Might*, low on fuel and shot up during a raid against Tokyo, strained to return to base on the island of Tinian in the distant Marianas. Unlike pilots in such a predicament before him, Lieutenant Fred Malo and his ten crew had an alternative that day; he headed for Iwo Jima and requested an emergency landing on one of the airfields.

When Iwo Jima came within sight, Malo dropped from the thick cloud cover and slapped down on the strip. A wing snapped a telephone pole as the big silver bomber came to a shuddering stop just 50ft from the end of the runway. Within half an hour, temporary repairs had been made, the fuel tanks were topped off, and the aircraft was airborne, headed once again for Tinian.

Dinah Might was the first of many crippled aircraft engaged in the strategic bombing campaign against Japan that found a temporary haven on Iwo Jima, and its crew were among an estimated 25,000 American airmen whose lives were probably saved when they avoided ditching in the Pacific Ocean.

wave, swarming ashore. However, most of the enemy gunners did not open fire. They had been instructed to wait until the beaches were literally choked with men and materiel.

Once conditions seemed favourable, the Japanese unleashed a torrent of fire on the Marines, who nevertheless struggled forward, their footing continually challenged by the unstable volcanic sand. They moved off the 3,000yds beachhead after taking an hour-long pummelling and losing 2,400 men on the first day alone. In the south, they succeeded in cutting off Mount Suribachi, a 554ft extinct volcano that dominated the island. On February 23, one of the most memorable moments of the Pacific War occurred with the raising of the US flag on the summit of Suribachi.

Still, a month of bitter combat lay ahead with the reserves of the 3rd Marine Division committed to the prolonged fight. Progress was measured in yards, and the odour of sulphur permeated the air. Marines fought the Japanese for control of otherwise nondescript rock formations and crags that gained infamous nicknames such as Turkey Knob, the Amphitheatre, Bloody Gorge, the Jungle of Stone and the Meat Grinder. Flamethrowers burned the defenders at their posts, and those who tried to escape were shot down in their tracks. Others were sealed alive in their cave fortresses as Marines used satchel charges and bulldozers to close the entrances forever.

At times, the Japanese launched massive Banzai suicide charges, flinging themselves toward entrenched Marine positions only to be mowed down in heaps. By February 27, all three airstrips were in American hands, but weeks of fighting remained. Not until March 26

Above: During the fighting at Iwo Jima, two American Marines turn a captured Japanese machine gun against the enemy. (US Marine Corps Archives via Wikimedia Commons)

Below left: US Landing Vehicle, Tracked (LVT) amphibious craft packed with Marines churn towards the beaches of Iwo Jima. (US Department of Defense via Wikimedia Commons)

Below right: Japanese General Tadamichi Kuribayashi executed a tenacious defence in depth at Iwo Jima. (Government of Japan via Wikimedia Commons)

MARINES RAISE FLAG ON MOUNT SURIBACHI

As fighting raged on the island of Iwo Jima, 25 riflemen of the 3rd Platoon, Company E, 2nd Battalion, 28th Marines – along with a few replacements from other Company E outfits that raised their number to 40 – moved out with orders to reach the summit of Mount Suribachi, the 554ft extinct volcano dominating the island. Under the command of 1st Lieutenant Harold G Schrier, the Marines picked their way forward. Japanese snipers took shots at them and individual enemy soldiers jumped up from spider holes. The Marines tossed grenades, fired into the mouths of caves and cut down the enemy soldiers lunging towards them.

Schrier's patrol, visible across the island and some distance out to sea as it snaked its way to the top of the mountain, had specific orders to raise the US flag, Old Glory – in this case a small example, 54 x 28in from the summit. Marine photographer Louis R Lowery recorded their progress, asking them to stop once and display the flag as he snapped the shutter of his camera.

Once they had fought their way to the crater, the Marines looked around for a suitable flagpole and found a length of pipe. Schrier and three other Marines lashed the flag to the pipe. At approximately 10.30am, the makeshift pole was planted and the small flag snapped in the breeze. The Marines below raised a cheer; whistles blew aboard ships.

General Holland Smith, commanding V Amphibious Corps, was escorting Secretary of the Navy James V Forrestal, who had journeyed to observe the operations. The secretary exclaimed: "The raising of that flag means a Marine Corps for another 500 years!"

About three hours after Schrier's patrol successfully completed its mission, Lieutenant Colonel Chandler Johnson, commander of the 2nd Battalion, 28th Marines, decided the original flag was too small and a runner was sent to the beach to find a larger one. He returned from the LST-779 with

A Marine maintains vigil after the raising of the first flag on Iwo Jima, February 23, 1945. (US Marine Corps via Wikimedia Commons)

This 7th War Loan Poster commemorates the epic flag-raising on Mount Suribachi. (US Government Printing Office via Wikimedia Commons)

Marines raise the US flag atop Mount Suribachi on Iwo Jima, February 23, 1945. (Associated Press News Joe Rosenthal US National Archives and Records Administration via Wikimedia Commons)

a replacement that measured 8 x 4ft8in. A second patrol delivered the flag to the summit of Suribachi and Associated Press photographer Joe Rosenthal decided to follow along.

When Rosenthal reached the crater, the raising of the second flag was already in progress. He tried not to obstruct the view of Marine William Genaust, filming with a movie camera. "Hey Bill! There it goes!" he yelled.

"Out of the corner of my eye, I had seen the men start the flag up," Rosenthal remembered. "I swung my camera around and shot the scene. That is how the picture was taken, and when you take a picture like that, you don't come away saying you got a great shot. You don't know."

Rosenthal had captured on film a moment that defined the courage and fortitude of the US Marine Corps and the will of a nation to see the war through to final victory. The image remains the most iconic symbol of the American fighting man in World War Two, and perhaps the most iconic war photograph ever taken. Summarising the character of the great battle, Admiral Chester Nimitz, at far-off Pearl Harbor, declared: "On Iwo island, uncommon valour was a common virtue."

Since the enduring photograph captured the second flag-raising, some observers declared that it had been staged. They were wrong. Rosenthal's film was flown to Guam and developed. Associated Press editor John Bodkin knew it was something special and said: "Here's one for all time!" He flashed the photo to the Associated Press office in New York and within 18 hours it was in distribution.

BATTLE OF MEIKTILA ENDS

Tanks and trucks of the British 62nd Motorised Brigade advance along a dirt road towards Meiktila. (Collections of the Imperial War Museums via Wikimedia Commons)

After defeating a Japanese offensive aimed at his 300-mile front stretching across the Plain of Imphal and establishing firm control of the city of Kohima, General William Slim and the British 14th Army concluded the decisive campaign of World War Two in Burma.

Slim had managed to inflict 6,000 casualties on the attacking Japanese at Kohima and withstood a lengthy siege with resupply by air at Imphal before the Indian 2nd and 5th Infantry Divisions cracked the enemy lines and opened the vital Imphal-Kohima road link. The Japanese were compelled to fall back towards the River Chindwin while Slim seized the initiative and kept the pressure on the faltering enemy.

By late 1944, Slim had chased the Japanese all the way to the banks of the Chindwin, and on January 14, 1945, he had unleashed the pivotal offensive of the war in the China-Burma-India Theatre. In early March, the 14th Army had taken the important communications centre of Meiktila; Japanese supply and communications links with the Burmese capital city of Rangoon were severed.

The British and Commonwealth offensive was aimed at crushing Japanese resistance in central Burma, protecting the long, recently established supply link to China called the Ledo Road, and set the stage for the liberation of the balance of Burma. The 14th Army attacked three Japanese armies under the command of General Hyotaro Kimura. The 33rd Corps struck towards Mandalay to draw Japanese attention while the 4th Corps moved as quietly as possible down the Gangaw and Kabaw Valleys of the mighty River Irrawaddy. They rolled forward on February 13 and forced the Japanese out of Meiktila on March 3.

With the fall of Meiktila, co-ordinated Japanese resistance in northern Burma disintegrated. On March 21, Slim's victorious forces completed a bitter struggle for Mandalay, ejecting the Japanese occupiers. By early April, the 36th Infantry Division arrived to support further operations in Burma, and Slim's troops fended off repeated Japanese counterattacks, forcing the Japanese to withdraw from central Burma along the banks of the swift-flowing Irrawaddy. With

the support of amphibious landings by the 15th Corps, the 33rd and 4th Corps executed a brilliant run to Rangoon before the onset of the monsoon season.

Historians have put forth that Slim's venture was one of the finest Allied land campaigns of World War Two. Slim was justifiably proud of his command and remarked: "Armies do not win wars by means of a few bodies of super-soldiers, but by the average quality of their standard units. Any well-trained infantry battalion should be able to do what a commando can do; in the 14th Army they could and did."

Indian troops of the Rajputana Rifles attack with armoured support in the drive to Meiktila. (Collections of the Imperial War Museums via Wikimedia Commons)

Infantrymen of the Punjab Rifles move forward towards Meiktila in company with an M4 Sherman medium tank. (Collections of the Imperial War Museums via Wikimedia Commons)

US FORCES CAPTURE BRIDGE AT REMAGEN

Above: Two towers of the Ludendorff Bridge are prominent in this photo taken March 11, 1945, from a tunnel on the east bank of the Rhine. (National Archives and Records Administration via Wikimedia Commons)

Left: Lieutenant Karl Timmerman led the American soldiers who seized the Ludendorff Bridge at Remagen. (US Army via Wikimedia Commons)

Startling reports filtered into higher headquarters of the US First Army, indicating that soldiers of the 9th Armored Division's 27th Armoured Infantry Regiment had located an intact bridge across the mighty River Rhine, the last great natural barrier between advancing Allied forces and the German Fatherland.

The desperate Nazi counterattack in the Battle of the Bulge had been beaten back in mid-January, so the First Army – under General Courtney Hodges – had resumed offensive operations. The Roer River dams had been taken and the bitter fighting of the Hürtgen Forest was a stinging, recent memory. Now the focus was on leaping the Rhine and blasting away at the black heart of the Third Reich. However, that ambitious objective required bridges, and even one that was intact across the Rhine would be a prize beyond measure.

Hodges had issued a standing order that read: "If such a bridge is found, exploit its use to the fullest and establish a bridgehead on the other side." Allied senior officers had discussed whether an intact bridge across the great river even existed – the Germans having displayed their skill at demolition, blowing up numerous spans to prevent their use by Allied spearheads.

The seizure of the Ludendorff railroad bridge across the Rhine at Remagen began early on the morning of March 7, 1945.

First Lieutenant Karl Timmerman, newly appointed commander of Company A, 27th Armored Infantry, had been summoned to the command post of the 14th Tank Battalion and informed that his company would lead the entire battalion advance to the banks of the Rhine.

At 11am, the infantrymen were hit by a German ambush and called up fire support in the form of a new M26 Pershing heavy tank mounting a burly 90mm main gun. The tank's fire rapidly quelled the

After its collapse on March 17, 1945, all that remained of the Ludendorff Bridge was a twisted mass of steel. (Franklin D Roosevelt Presidential Library and Museum via Wikimedia Commons)

Damaged by a demolition blast, the Ludendorff Bridge collapsed into the Rhine just four hours after this photo was taken. ((National Archives and Records Administration via Wikimedia Commons)

American soldiers gather at the edge of the Ludendorff railroad bridge, captured in March 1945. (Creative Commons Bundesarchiv Bild via Wikimedia Commons)

enemy resistance as several enemy soldiers put their hands in the air and others fled for their lives.

A short time later, Timmerman and company reached the Rhine, where he saw the Ludendorff Bridge, still standing, and realised the magnitude of his discovery. He sent the electrifying news up the chain of command and, at 1pm, General William M Hodge, commanding Combat Command B, 9th Armored Division, ordered Timmerman to move through the town of Remagen and take the bridge in a rapid movement supported by tank and small-arms fire from the west bank of the Rhine.

Timmerman stepped off at 3.20pm with 120 men and made the 'Follow me!' gesture with arm raised. German machine guns positioned in the towers at each end of the bridge began to chatter, and another from a post hidden in a half-submerged barge at the river's edge opened fire. American tanks fired at the defenders. Meanwhile, Timmerman had instructed about half his men to secure the western end of the bridge while the other half dashed to the eastern end and established a holding position there while providing covering fire. Quickly mounting their assault, the American soldiers advanced from steel girder to steel girder, German bullets pinging and ricocheting off the framework.

The Americans cut wires to charges planted by the Germans along the span and threw the solid explosives into the water below. One soldier remembered: "While we were running across the bridge… I spotted this lieutenant, standing out there completely exposed to the machine gun fire that was pretty heavy by this time. He was cutting wires and kicking the German demolition charges off the bridge with his feet!"

At approximately 3.40pm, a tremendous roar stopped Timmerman and his men in their tracks. In fact, everyone for some distance on either side of the bridge froze. German Major Hans Scheller had ordered the span blown up, but miraculously, as the shock wave dissipated and the smoke and

dust cleared, the bridge had lifted somewhat into the air and settled back down – still together. Soon, some American combat engineers reached the scene and began skilfully disarming the charges that remained.

Five minutes after the detonation, Sergeant Alexander Drabik became the first American soldier to reach the east bank of the Rhine. He had led his entire squad at a dead run over the entire 384ft length of the bridge, through the dust and debris of the explosion, and incredibly no man had suffered even a scratch.

Drabik remembered the hair-raising run sometime later: "We ran down the middle of the bridge, shouting as we went. I didn't stop because I knew that if I kept moving, they couldn't hit me. My men were in squad column and not one of them was hit. We took cover in some bomb craters. Then we just sat and waited for others to come. That's the way it was."

By 4pm, the Americans had secured both ends of the bridge, and others were working to fill a large blast crater at the western approach. Timmerman and his men established defensive positions on the eastern bank of the Rhine as best they could. Some German soldiers retreated immediately, while others were killed or wounded. More than 300 troops and a clutch of civilians were holed up in a nearby cave and soon surrendered.

With a stroke of luck and sheer audacity, American forces had secured their first opportunity to cross the Rhine with dry feet. For ten days the Ludendorff railroad bridge stood, and US troops and tanks took full advantage, even though the Germans tried to destroy it by air attack, artillery fire and even frogmen with demolition charges. Then, on March 17, amid the din of twisting steel, brick and concrete, the span collapsed into the river – another casualty of war.

An American soldier mans his quad .50-calibre anti-aircraft guns, with the Ludendorff Bridge prominent in the background. (US Army via Wikimedia Commons)

OPERATION MEETINGHOUSE: TOKYO FIREBOMBING

The Boeing B-29 Superfortress heavy bomber flew from bases in the Marianas during Operation Meetinghouse. (US Air Force via Wikimedia Commons)

The XXI Bomber Command, US Army Air Forces unleashed the most devastating air raid in military history as 334 Boeing B-29 Superfortress heavy bombers devastated Tokyo, the capital city of Japan.

Based on the islands of Guam and Tinian in the Mariana Archipelago, the Superfortresses were packed with incendiary bombs. In fact, General Curtis LeMay, in charge of XXI Bomber Command since January, had expressed dissatisfaction with the results of the strategic bombing of Japan to date. Early in his tenure, he railed: "This outfit is getting a lot of publicity without really accomplishing much." In response to the lacklustre performance, LeMay ordered the big bombers to be stripped of defensive weaponry and other equipment to make room for heavier incendiary bomb payloads. He further altered mission tactics, telling the bomber pilots to fly low into their targets rather than at high altitude in order to improve accuracy and hopefully render enemy anti-aircraft fire less effective.

Tokyo had been targeted by American bombers for the first time from the Marianas on November 24, 1944, when 88 Superfortresses of the 73rd Bombardment Wing attacked the Nakajima aircraft factory at Musashino in the suburbs of the city. Although the plant was a priority target believed to produce roughly 30 per cent of all aircraft engines in Japan, the results were poor. Only an estimated one per cent of the bombs dropped from high altitude had found their mark. The B-29s returned to Tokyo three days later, hitting dockyards and manufacturing facilities. They struck the Japanese capital five more times prior to the fateful night of March 9, 1945.

LeMay's bombing plan was chilling in conception. Dubbed Operation Meetinghouse, the massed mighty B-29s would fly low, releasing their incendiaries in a concentrated area. The resulting fires would no doubt begin to consume the surrounding structures, largely built of wood. The conflagration would grow in intensity, soon overwhelming fire control units and laying waste to wide swaths of residential and industrial areas alike.

LeMay's tactical revisions had been tested earlier, but on this night their destructive capability was starkly revealed. The largest Marianas-based air assault to date against the home islands of Japan was set in motion as three full air wings of B-29s took off and proceeded through darkening skies towards Tokyo. Pathfinder aircraft led the way, marking the target with their own incendiaries that painted a gigantic 'X' of flame to guide the waves of follow-on attackers.

Then, flying at altitudes of just 5,000 to 9,000ft, the waves of Superfortresses followed, delivering 1,665 tons of explosives. Their principal weapons were the 500-pound E-46 cluster bomb, which held 38 M-69 bomblets containing the jellied gasoline mixture known as napalm, and the 100lb M-47 incendiary, which carried napalm and white phosphorous. The B-29 pilots were instructed to drop their payloads at 50ft intervals, depositing an estimated 25 tons of ordnance per square mile on the city of Tokyo. Of the 334 bombers designated for the raid, 279 initially reached the target area in the northwest quadrant of the city.

This photo of the bleak landscape in Tokyo was taken in August 1945, just as the war was ending. (US Army Signal Corps via Wikimedia Commons)

Leaflets like this were dropped over Tokyo prior to the firebombing raids, encouraging civilians to leave the city. (US Government via Wikimedia Commons)

The Ningyocho district of Tokyo was devastated by the firebombing of Operation Meetinghouse. (Government of Japan via Wikimedia Commons)

A wide area of Tokyo is consumed in flames during a US Army Air Forces raid in May 1945. (US Army via Wikimedia Commons)

Some bombers were blown off course by strong prevailing winds, while some navigators became disorientated amid adverse weather conditions. A few of these aircraft corrected their courses and eventually found Tokyo, but in the meantime 226 B-29s rained bombs on the city during the first two hours of the raid.

Air raid sirens wailed, and residents were woken by a burgeoning inferno. The densely populated working-class districts of Tokyo's Chuo and Koto wards, not far from the crowded port facilities, bore the brunt of the attack. The M-46 munitions were fused to release their M-69 bomblets at altitudes of 2,000 to 2,500ft. The bomblets crashed through the tin roofs of buildings and homes and exploded on the ground and in the streets. In three to five seconds, they began emitting fiery jets of napalm that rapidly engulfed nearby flammable materials. the M-47s exploded on impact. Together, these incendiaries spread fires to structures in the surrounding congested area, fusing into a single torrent of flame, whipped by winds and producing a terrifying firestorm.

Buffeted by high winds, some of which were actually caused by the conflagration below that generated its own super-heated updrafts, 27 Superfortresses were lost in the raid, 14 to anti-aircraft fire and 13 to mechanical failures. Three B-29 pilots became disorientated and crashed into a mountainside. But as the bombers turned for home, they left in their wake an unfolding debacle of unprecedented scale.

Altogether, 282 bombers eventually found Tokyo and, when the flames finally subsided fully, 16 square miles of the Japanese capital had been laid waste. People panicked, fleeing their burning homes but finding no respite in the shadowy streets. Some observers asserted that the water in nearby canals reached boiling point. While estimates of casualties vary widely, the US Strategic Bombing Survey concluded that 88,000 people, mostly civilians, had perished in the flames while 41,000 more were injured. About a million were left homeless, their dwellings reduced to piles of ash. Before World War Two in the Pacific ended, the American bombers returned to Tokyo more than half a dozen times, and at least 17 raids hit the city during the conflict.

Controversy surrounds the massive Operation Meetinghouse raid to this day as historians wrestle with the question of meting out such destruction to a civilian population. Regardless, there is no question that the raid struck a telling blow to Japanese morale and probably hastened the end of the war in the Pacific. Emperor Hirohito toured the devastated area and was said to have been visibly moved. And in the final analysis, General LeMay had seen total war for what it is – an ugly and humanly degrading business.

General Curtis LeMay was the architect of the strategic bombing that devastated Japanese cities. (US Air Force via Wikimedia Commons)

JAPANESE BOMBS STRIKE USS *FRANKLIN*

Heavily damaged, the aircraft carrier USS *Franklin* approaches New York harbour on April 26, 1945. (US Navy via Wikimedia Commons)

A lone Japanese aeroplane – its actual type unknown – eluded combat air patrols and avoided radar detection, flying low to drop a pair of 551lb bombs on the Essex-class aircraft carrier USS *Franklin*. Heroic efforts to bring fires under control and save the great ship were eventually successful, but *Franklin* had been seriously damaged; 724 people were killed and 265 wounded.

The unfortunate attack occurred while *Franklin* and other US Navy aircraft carriers were conducting operations off the Japanese home islands. Raids against staging areas and military targets in Japan were a prelude to the American amphibious landings on the island of Okinawa, scheduled to get under way 12 days later. By the spring of 1945, US Navy warships operated regularly in close proximity to Japan in order to disrupt the flow of supplies and reinforcements to islands that would later become battlegrounds.

Captain Stephen Jurika, Jr, the navigator aboard *Franklin*, later recalled: "The mission of our task force was to raid Japanese airfields in Kyushu, Shikoku and western Honshu, from which we expected all the Japanese aircraft would be launched against the Okinawa invasion, and, in truth, that's what happened. The launch point for our aircraft was 45 miles off the mainland of Honshu. It would take our fighters and bombers somewhere between 20 and 30 minutes from time of launch to arrive at enemy airfields."

Damage control parties battle smoke and flames aboard the aircraft carrier USS *Franklin*, struck by two bombs off the home islands of Japan. (US Navy via Wikimedia Commons)

The stricken aircraft carrier USS *Franklin* billows smoke as the cruiser USS *Santa Fe* comes close alongside to render aid. (US Navy via Wikimedia Commons)

Like other carriers in Task Force 58.2, *Franklin's* flight deck was periodically packed with aircraft preparing for take-off. However, *Franklin* was the only carrier with aircraft being armed with a new weapon, the 11.75in Tiny Tim rocket, specially designed to hit ground targets. Jurika remembered that on the morning of the 19th, five or six airplanes had just taken off from *Franklin's* flight deck when the unexpected Japanese attack occurred: "I saw this out of the corner of my eye," he said, "and I saw two bombs drop from the plane and hit just forward of the forward elevator, and within a fraction of a second, of course, an enormous explosion took place down below, and the elevator lifted up, cockeyed…"

The Japanese bombs penetrated to the hangar deck and exploded, cooking off Tiny Tim rockets that slithered across the deck and through the gaping hole left by the blasted elevator. Bombs and torpedoes detonated in the searing flames. Power was lost, and *Franklin* listed 15° to starboard. Smoke billowed from the blazing interior of the carrier as the cruiser *Santa Fe* came alongside to render aid. The cruiser *Pittsburgh* then took *Franklin* in tow until boilers were operational and the stricken carrier could generate its own power again.

Franklin limped to Ulithi for temporary repairs and then undertook a 12,000-mile odyssey to Pearl Harbor, through the Panama Canal and finally to the Brooklyn Navy Yard, reaching New York 40 days after the Japanese bombs had ravaged the ship. No Essex-class aircraft carriers were lost to enemy action during World War Two, but *Franklin*, indeed, came nearest.

LIBERATION OF MANDALAY

With the inception of his 14th Army campaign to drive the Japanese from Burma, control the vital Burma Road supply route and liberate the capital city of Rangoon, General William Slim determined that the Japanese intended to move away from defensive positions along the River Chindwin and decided to strike towards the communications centre of Meiktila.

To facilitate his offensive, in January 1945 Slim issued orders to advance on Mandalay, the second-largest city in Burma, situated on the east bank of the River Irrawaddy. The movement was intended to divert Japanese attention from his objective at Meiktila, which fell to British and Commonwealth troops on March 3. Meanwhile, the Japanese defence of Mandalay was determined, but after weeks of fighting the city finally fell.

Supported by armour, the Indian 19th Infantry Division was tasked with taking Mandalay from the north. Arriving on the outskirts of the city in late January, the division encountered stiff resistance from the Japanese 15th Division, contesting its bridgeheads across the Irrawaddy. By the end of February, the Japanese retired to a defence line that ran from the area of Mandalay Hill in the north across the Irrawaddy to the Mandalay Canal east of the city. Positions at Mandalay Hill, the Pagoda fields and Fort Dufferin were heavily fortified.

The 19th Division formed a mobile striking unit called Stiletto Force, which was ordered to advance rapidly on the heights of the 934ft Mandalay Hill. Stiletto Force moved forward on March 5 and soon encountered stiff resistance, contrary to reports that only a relative few enemy troops were defending the area. Four days later, elements of the 4th Gurkha Rifles seized the highest point on Mandalay Hill and repelled Japanese counterattacks. Heavy fighting then required reinforcements to clear tunnels and strongpoints before Mandalay Hill was declared secure on March 12.

Major General T W Rees, commander of the 19th Indian Division, enters Fort Dufferin at Mandalay. (Collections of the Imperial War Museums via Wikimedia Commons)

Indian soldiers, one with a Bren light machine gun, fire from positions near pagodas on Mandalay Hill. (Collections of the Imperial War Museums via Wikimedia Commons)

Soldiers of the 19th Indian Division accompanied by an M3 Lee Tank pause during the fighting at Mandalay. (Collections of the Imperial War Museums via Wikimedia Commons)

While fighting raged on Mandalay Hill, elements of the Frontier Force Regiment reached the north wall of Fort Dufferin to the south. The 28ft-high wall was breached on March 9 and efforts to take the citadel began in earnest the next day. However, the defenders clung tenaciously to their positions, beating back successive attacks for more than a week. On the 18th, the Japanese commander received orders to evacuate the city, and two days later Mandalay was in British hands. The Indian 19th Division was soon released to join the main thrust towards Rangoon.

OPERATION PLUNDER BEGINS

After lengthy preparations, marshalling troops and supplies, Field Marshal Bernard Montgomery, commander of the Allied 21st Army Group, initiated Operation Plunder, the crossing of the River Rhine in the north of the broad front offensive into the Fatherland of Nazi Germany.

Although Allied forces had managed crossings in two areas to the south, the main thrust of the offensive as planned by General Dwight D Eisenhower, Supreme Commander of Allied Forces in Western Europe, charged Montgomery with crossing the great natural barrier, serving as the main axis of advance, cutting off the Ruhr – Germany's industrial heartland – thus hastening the end of World War Two in Europe.

Montgomery's XXI Army Group consisted of the British Second Army, US Ninth Army and Canadian First Army, a massive force of nearly 1.3 million combat and support troops. In early March, he wrote in a letter to his son, David: "I am busy getting ready for the next battle. The Rhine is some river, but we shall get over it."

True to form, Montgomery spent weeks building up his forces, leaving as little to chance as possible. Dubbed Operation Plunder, the crossing of the Rhine involved the movement of many soldiers directly to the east bank of the river aboard amphibious personnel carriers called 'Buffaloes'. A massive airborne component, Operation Varsity, was scheduled to launch shortly after the ground component was initiated.

American soldiers of the 89th Infantry Division crouch low in their amphibious craft while crossing the Rhine during Operation Plunder. (US Army via Wikimedia Commons)

Air bombardment hit German targets, particularly the dispositions of Colonel General Johannes Blaskowitz's Army Group H and his subordinate 1st Parachute Army under General Alfred Schlemm. Despite taking serious casualties, Schlemm had expressed confidence that his tough troops could hold the east bank of the Rhine: "First Parachute Army succeeded in withdrawing all of its supply elements in orderly fashion, saving almost all its artillery, and withdrawing enough troops so that a new defensive front can be built up on the east bank."

Meanwhile, Montgomery devised his plan for Operation Plunder, centred on the town of Wesel in western Germany. After a preparatory artillery barrage from more than 5,000 big guns, hauled forward to pound the enemy along the riverbank and well beyond, the 51st Highland Division and 9th Canadian Brigade of General Brian Horrocks' XXX Corps crossed the river aboard the Buffaloes on March 23 – soon followed by the 43rd Wessex Division, 3rd Infantry Division, the Guards Armoured Division and a pair of armoured brigades.

In the predawn hours of the following day, the 15th Scottish Division crossed the Rhine near the village of Xanten, roughly halfway between Wesel and the town of Rees to the northwest. Once the 15th Division, a component of General Neil Ritchie's XII Corps, had established a lodgement on the east bank of the Rhine, engineers threw a Bailey bridge across the 400yd-wide

Above: The German town of Wesel lies in ruins after Allied air and artillery bombardment in preparation for Operation Plunder. (US Army Air Forces via Wikimedia Commons)

Below: A 3in mortar team of the 8th Royal Scots fires its weapon at German positions on March 24, 1945. (Collections of the Imperial War Museums via Wikimedia Commons)

British Commandos fire heavy machine guns at German positions on the outskirts of Wesel. (Collections of the Imperial War Museums via Wikimedia Commons)

soon as possible. Over the Rhine, then, let us go. And good hunting to you on the other side."

Indeed, German forces put up stiff resistance at several locations around Wesel, and the 7th Battalion, Black Watch, of the 154th Brigade encountered strong German defences at Bienen, north of Rees, where the 9th Canadian Infantry Brigade came to its relief. Some German armoured counterattacks were repelled, while the American 30th and 79th Infantry Divisions sustained light casualties south of Wesel, where accurate artillery fire had disrupted the enemy response. The airborne component fought pitched battles with the Germans, but managed to beat back counterattacks and disrupted enemy communications and troop movements in the process.

Within 72 hours, the Allied bridgehead across the Rhine was well established, expanding nearly 30 miles from the east bank of the great river on a 25-mile front.

With Operation Plunder well under way, Prime Minister Winston Churchill and numerous senior Allied military officers stride ashore on the east bank of the Rhine. (Collections of the Imperial War Museums via Wikimedia Commons)

waterway. The tanks of the 11th Armoured Division then rolled forward, poised to execute a breakthrough of the enemy defences.

Again within hours, two divisions of the Allied First Airborne Army, the British 6th and the American 17th, boarded their Douglas C-47/Dakota transport aircraft to execute Operation Varsity. The airborne phase of the great Rhine crossing included 21,680 paratroopers and glidermen riding and parachuting into German rear areas to support the ground offensive aboard 1,696 aeroplanes and 1,348 gliders.

Montgomery addressed his troops before Operation Plunder: "The 21st Army Group will now cross the Rhine. The enemy possibly thinks he is safe behind this great river obstacle. We all agree that it is a great obstacle; but we will show the enemy that he is far from safe behind it. This great Allied fighting machine, composed of integrated land and air forces, will deal with the problem in no uncertain manner. And having crossed the Rhine, we will crack about in the plains of northern Germany, chasing the enemy from pillar to post. The swifter and more energetic our action, the sooner the war will be over, and that is what we all desire; to get on with the job and finish off the German war as

Clouds of Allied paratroopers plummet earthwards during Operation Varsity, the airborne component of Operation Plunder. (US Army Signal Corps via Wikimedia Commons)

US FORCES LAND ON OKINAWA

Knocked out by Japanese fire, a pair of US M4 Sherman medium tanks lies abandoned on Okinawa. (US Army via Wikimedia Commons)

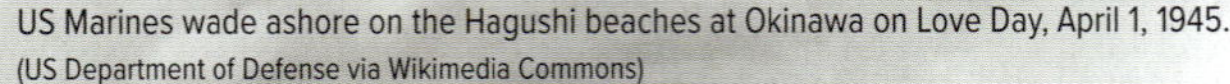

US Marines wade ashore on the Hagushi beaches at Okinawa on Love Day, April 1, 1945. (US Department of Defense via Wikimedia Commons)

reached immense proportions as 1,300 ships of every description assembled offshore and 750,000 tons of supplies were stockpiled to support the invasion.

The Okinawa campaign was placed in the hands of US Army General Simon Boliver Buckner, Jr, son of an American Civil War general. Buckner commanded the X Army, which consisted of the III Marine Amphibious Corps, under General Roy S Geiger, and the XXIV Army Corps, led by General John S Hodge. The US Fifth Fleet was commanded by Admiral Raymond A Spruance, while Admiral Richmond Kelly Turner was in charge of all amphibious forces in the Pacific theatre. The III Amphibious Corps included the 1st and 6th Marine Divisions with the 2nd Marine Division in reserve, while the XXIV Army Corps comprised the 7th, 77th and 96th Infantry Divisions, the 27th Division in reserve. Many of the assault troops were veterans of earlier fighting.

One Marine crouches while another fires his Thompson submachine gun across the barren landscape of Okinawa at Wana Ridge. (US Army via Wikimedia Commons)

The curious convergence of April Fool's Day and Easter Sunday was lost on no one in 1945, and neither was the significance of April 1 during World War Two in the Pacific.

Designated Love Day, or L-Day, to avoid confusion with the D-Day landings that had taken place on the other side of the world in French Normandy on June 6, 1944, the target for Operation Iceberg was the island of Okinawa in the Ryukyu archipelago. Situated just 340 miles from the Japanese home island of Kyushu, Allied commanders were convinced that Okinawa should be taken as a staging area for troops and supplies in anticipation of an invasion of Japan itself, as well as to eliminate the island as a base for Japanese air and naval resistance.

During the week prior to L-Day, American warships fired 13,000 shells at Japanese positions on Okinawa, while naval aircraft flew 3,095 sorties to soften up the defences. As the naval bombardment continued, amphibious landing craft churned towards the Hagushi beaches on the southwestern shore of the island. Preparations had

General Buckner's plan called for a rapid advance off the beaches while a feint was executed in the southeast to draw Japanese attention away from the actual landing area. Once ashore, the American forces were to drive eastward, directly across Okinawa, capture two vital airfields, Kadena and Yontan, split the island in two and then turn north and south to destroy enemy resistance and take control of the length and breadth of Okinawa.

Opposing the Americans were 100,000 army and naval troops of the Japanese 9th, 24th and 62nd Divisions along with the understrength 44th Independent Mixed Brigade and 15th Independent Mixed Regiment under General Mitsuru Ushijima. An advocate of defence in depth, Ushijima prepared three extensive lines of resistance in the south, and intended to exact a heavy toll on the invaders, buying time for further defensive preparations in the home islands.

On L-Day, Ushijima held his fire, watching 16,000 American troops swarm ashore in an hour. By the end of the day, 60,000 US soldiers and Marines were ashore, and the beachhead extended 5,000yds inland and 15,000yds wide. There were few casualties. However, it was the calm before the storm.

Early progress was swift as both airfields were captured on the first day. After four days, the Americans had taken territory estimated to have required three weeks of combat to secure. Okinawa was, in fact, cut in half by April 3, and American aircraft had begun operating from Kadena and Yontan. The US flag was raised at the extreme northern tip of Okinawa on April 13, but the intensity of the combat to the south increased exponentially. The 7th and 96th Divisions struck Ushijima's first major line of resistance on April 19, and soon the reserve 27th Division was committed. After three horrific weeks, Ushijima ordered the survivors out of his first line, pulling them back to the fortified Shuri Line, dominated by the ancient Shuri Castle, where four Marine divisions struck beginning in early May across a 9,000yd front.

Meanwhile, the US ships offshore endured almost continual attacks from Japanese Kamikaze suicide aircraft. The damage inflicted during ten mass sorties or Kikusui (Floating Chrysanthemum), some numbering up to 350 aircraft, was horrific. On April 23, Fleet Admiral Chester Nimitz,

Smoke and flames billow above the flight deck of USS *Bunker Hill* after the carrier was struck by two Kamikaze suicide aircraft off Okinawa on May 11, 1945. (US Navy via Wikimedia Commons)

Commander-in-Chief Pacific, flew to Okinawa to rouse Buckner's pace and minimise the losses. The fleet remained on station, suffering 4,907 killed or missing and 29 ships sunk with 120 damaged before their ordeal ended. One of the most devastating attacks occurred on May 11, when the aircraft carrier *Bunker Hill* was hit by two Kamikazes and turned into a blazing pyre during its 58th day on station.

The assault on the Shuri Line was brutal. Names like Wana Ridge, Wana Draw, Dakeshi Ridge, Conical Hill, Half Moon, Horseshoe and Sugar Loaf became legendary for the bloody fighting that occurred. The 22nd Marine Regiment lost 400 men, nearly half their number, in three days. At Sugar Loaf alone, the 6th Marine Division absorbed nearly 2,700 casualties. Ushijima did not abandon the Shuri Line until the end of May. His last line, from Kunishi Ridge to Hills 89 and 95, was held until the island was declared secure on June 22, 1945, after 82 days of fighting. Four days earlier, General Buckner had been killed by a Japanese shell and General Geiger had taken temporary command.

The harvest of death at Okinawa was incredible. American combat casualties on the island totalled 7,374 killed, 31,807 wounded and 239 missing. The Japanese garrison was decimated with only 11,000 prisoners taken; the others had perished along with more than 2,700 Kamikaze pilots who had plunged to their deaths. Approximately 150,000 Okinawan civilians died, too. It was the longest battle of the Pacific War and American planners looked to a prospective invasion of the Japanese home islands with understandable dread.

Lieutenant Colonel Richard P Ross, Jr, commander of 3rd Battalion, 1st Marines, risks enemy sniper fire to plant the US flag atop Shuri Castle. (US Department of Defense via Wikimedia Commons)

Moments before he was killed by a Japanese artillery shell, General Buckner peers across the Okinawan landscape. (US Marine Corps via Wikimedia Commons)

SOVIET FORCES LAUNCH VIENNA OFFENSIVE

Two Soviet soldiers assist a wounded comrade through a rubble-strewn street in embattled Vienna. (Government of the Russian Federation Yevgeny Khaldei via Wikimedia Commons)

After weeks of costly fighting through Hungary and blunting the last German offensive of World War Two, the troops and tanks of the Soviet 2nd and 3rd Ukrainian Fronts launched their direct assault on the city of Vienna, the famed capital of Austria and centre of the Ostmark region of the greater German Reich since the Anschluss (annexation) of 1938.

In the south of the broad Red Army front line, the Soviets committed roughly a million troops to the advance toward the Austrian frontier and sustained nearly a half million casualties, including 140,000 killed or captured. In the process, Marshal Fyodor Tolbukhin's 2nd Ukrainian Front and the 3rd Ukrainian Front, under General Rodion Malinovsky, made significant westward progress, Tolbukhin's command moving smartly along both banks of the River Danube.

As the Soviets were poised to launch their offensive against Vienna, the Germans unleashed Operation Spring Awakening, hoping to slow the inexorable advance of their sworn enemy. From March 6-15, The 3rd Ukrainian Front absorbed the brunt of the Nazi attacks, which petered out mid-month and did little to dissuade the Red Army. With the end of Spring Awakening, the Nazis lost vital oil reserves in eastern Europe and found themselves again on the receiving end of the Soviet juggernaut.

On April 2, Tolbukhin launched the Vienna Offensive. Early attacks by Malinovsky's forces secured the southern flank of the 3rd Ukrainian Front, approaching Vienna from the south and reaching the suburbs of the city within 48 hours. Manoeuvring to besiege the city, the 4th and 9th Guards Armies, 6th Guards Tank Army and 46th Army primarily faced General Wilhelm Bittrich's II SS Panzer Corps, while the defences of the city were under the direct command of General Rudolf von Bünau.

After five days of street fighting, the Soviets battered their way into the eastern and southern suburbs of Vienna, and by April 8 the 6th Guards Tank Army and 9th Guards Army fought their way towards the city centre from the west, where the main railway terminal was a significant objective. Once the heart of Vienna was in their sights, the Soviets struck bridges and canal areas along the Danube. Several spans were destroyed, but some crossings remained intact. The Germans defended the Floridsdorf Bridge to the last, sacrificing a detachment of the 2nd SS Division Das Reich in the task.

While street fighting continued in the Austrian capital, Tolbukhin ordered some units to bypass Vienna and advance toward the cities of Linz and Graz. Meanwhile, the urban warfare began to subside by April 15 and the city was declared secure on that date. In the wake of the battle, utilities were smashed and many buildings reduced to rubble. During the month preceding the fall of Vienna, the Red Army lost an estimated 155,000 casualties, roughly 30,000 of them killed in action. German losses were approaching 168,000.

From Vienna, the Soviets pursued the retreating Germans towards another patchwork defence line on the route to the Fatherland itself. Politically, the Soviets saw territorial gains in eastern Europe as an expansion of their sphere of influence and a bargaining chip with the Western Allies. Vienna, like Berlin, was divided into four occupation zones during post-war administration.

Left: Marshal Fyodor Tolbukhin led the Red Army's 3rd Ukrainian Front in the capture of Vienna. (Creative Commons Ministry of Defence of the Russian Federation via Wikimedia Commons)

Below: Soviet troops relax while riding trucks bound for Vienna, April 1945. (Government of Ukraine via Wikimedia Commons)

GERMAN FORCES SURROUNDED IN THE RUHR

From the inception of the Western Allies' ground campaign against Nazi forces in France and the Low Countries, the occupation of the Ruhr – the industrial heart of Germany – had been a priority. The capture of the Ruhr was expected to largely deny the enemy its ability to supply and maintain armed forces in the field.

On this date, the end of Nazi resistance in the Ruhr took a major step forward as troops and tanks of the US First and Ninth Armies linked up at Lippstadt, Germany, surrounding Field Marshal Walter Model's Army Group B. After bridging the great River Rhine at multiple points, the Allied 21st Army Group under Field Marshal Bernard Montgomery, and 12th Army Group commanded by General Omar Bradley, pursued their plan of encirclement: The Ninth Army, under General William Simpson, crossing the river near Wesel during the 21st Army Group's Operation Plunder, and the First Army, commanded by General Courtney Hodges, exploiting the capture of the intact Ludendorff railroad bridge at Remagen to initially reach the east bank of the Rhine.

The First Army swung northeast in late March, while the Ninth turned southeast to constitute a large pincer movement, rapidly threatening to trap about 370,000 German soldiers, approximately 19 divisions including troops, tanks and irreplaceable equipment. Once the jaws of the pincer were closed, the majority of the Allied forces east of the Rhine continued their rapid thrust into the German Fatherland. However, 18 US divisions were detailed to complete the reduction of what became known as the Ruhr Pocket.

The US 75th Division, Ninth Army, and 95th Division, detailed from the US Third Army, advanced near Dortmund and blunted a German counterattack during five days of heavy fighting from April 4-9. To the south, the defenders used rugged terrain to their advantage, delaying attacks from the three infantry divisions of the US III Corps, the 2nd, 80th and 99th. Elements of the US 17th Airborne and British 6th Airborne Divisions were also engaged. Allied tactical air strikes punished the Germans, restricting troop and supply movements during daylight hours.

By April 10, the city of Essen, nexus of the famed Krupp steelworks and munitions manufacturing, fell to the Ninth Army and, four days later, another link-up with First Army split the Ruhr Pocket in half, east and west. German unit cohesion began to fray as communications were lost and the remnants of the 15th Army surrendered en masse on April 14. Model, an ardent Nazi, chose to disband the Army Group B command structure rather than surrender, and by April 16, organised resistance had collapsed with the surrender of the eastern enclave. The reduction of German positions in the west was declared complete two days later.

Allied casualties included 1,500 killed and 8,000 wounded during the 18-day operation, while the disastrous defeat cost the Germans 317,000 prisoners and about 10,000 dead.

At a holding facility near Remagen, Germany, a US soldier stands guard over hundreds of prisoners captured in the Ruhr, April 25, 1945. (US Army via Wikimedia Commons)

Top: Soldiers of the US 8th Infantry Division, First Army, advance into dense forest to attack a German position near the town of Siegen, April 6, 1945. (US Army Signal Corps Archive via Wikimedia Commons)

Right: An American medic, with the assistance of a German nurse, tends a German prisoner wounded during the fighting in the Ruhr. (US Army Signal Corps Archive via Wikimedia Commons)

The great battleship *Yamato* ploughs through Japanese coastal waters during sea trials in October 1941. (Government of Japan via Wikimedia Commons)

JAPANESE SUPER BATTLESHIP *YAMATO* SUNK

During her final sortie, a suicide run during Operation Ten-Go – the Japanese effort to destroy American forces attempting to seize the island of Okinawa – the Imperial Navy super battleship *Yamato* was swarmed by nearly 400 US Navy carrier-based aircraft and sunk, with the loss of 2,498 crew from a complement of 2,700.

Along with sister ship *Musashi, Yamato* was the largest battleship ever built. Launched on August 8, 1940, and entering service on December 16, 1941, the massive battleship displaced nearly 73,000 tons fully loaded for combat. Her main armament consisted of nine 18.1in Type 94 naval guns along her centreline and amidships. Other armament included 6.1in and 5in guns along with an array of anti-aircraft mounts. During the epic Battle of Leyte Gulf in October 1944, *Yamato* had served as the flagship of the Japanese Centre Force, nearly succeeding in disrupting the American landings in the Philippines.

However, by the spring of 1945, her mission was one-way only. Ordered to beach between Higashi and Yomitan and use her heavy guns to bombard the American landing zones on Okinawa, *Yamato* and her escorts sortied from the port facilities at Tokuyama on April 6, 1945, sailing into the combat zone. The following day, she was set upon by dive bombers and torpedo airplanes launched from the aircraft carriers USS *Intrepid*, USS *Langley*, USS *Bennington* and USS *Yorktown* of Task Group 58.4, among others.

Piloting a Curtiss SB2C Helldiver dive bomber flying from *Bennington's* deck, Lieutenant (Junior Grade) Edward Sieber spotted the mammoth enemy battleship and years later recalled his attack: "We were in a 90° dive and I was getting ready for a salvo, shooting everything at once – eight rockets, 20mm cannon, two 500lb bombs and two 1,000lb semi-armour-piercing bombs. Then I pulled out. A dive takes less than a minute, but you'd be surprised how long a minute can be. I thought I hit the No. 3 turret. We probably hit a turret. I know we created havoc."

Sieber later received the Navy Cross for heroism in pressing home his attack against *Yamato*.

The American air assault began at 12.37pm and continued unabated for two hours. At least ten bombs and seven torpedoes struck home. Several torpedoes impacted on Yamato's port side, causing a heavy list. The ship was wracked by internal explosions, capsized and sank to the bottom of the Pacific in 1,200ft of water about 50 miles southwest of the Japanese home island of Kyushu.

Left: During the last moments of *Yamato*, an ammunition magazine erupts as the battleship plunges beneath the waves. (US Navy via Wikimedia Commons)

Right: After sustaining damage during the Battle of Leyte Gulf, *Yamato* continues toward a surface engagement off Samar, Philippines. (US Government via Wikimedia Commons)

OPERATION AMHERST

Free French and British troopers of the Special Air Service (SAS) concluded a daring raid behind German lines in the Netherlands to take control of bridges, canals and airfields ahead of advancing Allied ground forces. The Germans were retreating before the Allied ground spearheads following the crossing of the River Rhine in March, so the opportunity was ripe for such an operation. The venture was tied to the progress of the Canadian First Army, under General Henry D G Crerar, tasked with the liberation of the northern Netherlands and protecting the western flank of the British Second Army, then driving into western Germany.

Under the command of Brigadier Mike Calvert – who earned fame in the China-Burma-India theatre at the head of 77 Brigade – 700 men of the French 3rd and 4th SAS parachuted into the Dutch countryside in the northwest of the province of Drenthe on the night of April 7, while another contingent came down in southeast Friesland, near the border with Drenthe, and made contact with Dutch resistance fighters in the vicinity of the village of Appelscha. Captain Pierre Sicaud led the French SAS and parachuted with the second group, seriously injuring an eye during his descent.

The jump was made in adverse weather conditions, particularly thick cloud cover that prevented the SAS from exiting their aircraft at the normal altitude of just over 800ft. Instead, they were obliged to hit the silk at about 2,000ft, which caused a dispersal over a wide area. Among the 46 distinct groups airlifted, only 17 descended within their assigned drop zones.

A third French group was deposited near the town of Haulerwijk, just over six miles from Appelscha. This clutch of SAS men was detected by German patrols on the morning of

In this October 1945 photo, Brigadier Mike Calvert reviews the assembled French 3rd and 4th SAS. (Collections of the Imperial War Museums via Wikimedia Commons)

April 8, and a brisk firefight developed. One Frenchman was killed and others were captured. However, a few managed to escape the German dragnet and slipped away into the nearby forest. Meanwhile, the other SAS members conducted quick attacks on German posts, inflicting casualties and then melting into the surrounding woods with the help of a Dutch agent returning to his homeland to lead the parachutists through familiar territory.

The SAS conducted a reconnaissance of a small airfield at Steenwijk, finding extensive bomb damage inflicted by Allied aircraft that would render the facility unusable for an extended period. Among other attacks, they hit manufacturing centres and a bridge at Orvelte and Oranje, calling in air support from RAF Hawker Tempest fighter bombers on a selected basis.

The Germans were confused at first, but regrouped to counterattack, inflicting some casualties on the SAS before the Canadian 8th Reconnaissance Regiment, vanguard of Crerar's command, came to their relief. The SAS suffered 34 killed, 60 wounded and 68 captured, an overall casualty rate of more than 23%. German casualties totalled nearly 500.

Left: Captain Pierre Sicaud was seriously injured during the Operation Amherst parachute drop. (Creative Commons Bruno Sicaud via Wikimedia Commons)

Below: This monument at Assen, Netherlands, commemorates the heroism of the French SAS who participated in Operation Amherst. (Creative Commons Sander Knol via Wikimedia Commons)

SOVIETS CAPTURE KÖNIGSBERG

Supported by an SU-76 self-propelled assault gun, Soviet infantrymen attack at Königsberg. (Government of the Russian Federation via Wikimedia Commons)

After more than 1.5 million Soviet troops knifed into East Prussia in mid-January 1945, and virtually isolated the provincial capital of Königsberg, trapping the German 3rd Panzer Army and approximately 200,000 civilians, the Red Army concluded a four-day direct assault on the city's defences and compelled General Otto Lasch to surrender what remained of the German forces.

During the three-month siege of Königsberg, fighting erupted sporadically as the Germans attempted to maintain a link to the port of Pillau on the Baltic Sea. At the same time, Soviet spearheads bypassed the city and proceeded towards Berlin as the 3rd Belorussian Front – under Marshal Aleksandr Vasilevsky – tightened the noose. However, the Germans had fortified the city and the surrounding Samland peninsula, having taken a heavy toll during the earlier Red Army advance, which had been slowed at times to a crawl.

Although the urgency to capture Königsberg ebbed with the advance of Soviet forces further westward, the situation for the civilians inside the city remained desperate. During the winter months some attempted to cross the iced-over Vistula Lagoon to Pillau and perhaps escape by sea, while others chose to remain and endure the privations of the siege. In early April, the Soviet high command, Stavka, ordered Vasilevsky to take the city by direct assault.

The Soviets realised that such an attack would be costly and relied on repeated air attacks combined with a sustained artillery barrage to pound the German defensive positions. In some locations, the Soviet heavy guns were concentrated to more than 155 weapons per mile, and the preparatory avalanche of shells lasted four days. The Soviet forces advanced on two main axes intent on pressuring the defenders at multiple points. To the north, the 39th and 49th Armies were

positioned to attack, and in the south the 11th Guards Army was poised to strike. To the northeast, the 50th Army contributed two corps to the assault while a third corps maintained the integrity of the Soviet front line.

To reach the centre of Königsberg, the Soviets were obliged to breach concentric German defensive lines. The assault got under way in the north at dawn on April 6, and two German lines were defeated by noon before resistance stiffened, particularly along the western edge of the city. In the south, the assault stepped off after a three-hour artillery bombardment. By mid-afternoon, reserves had been committed, but two German lines had been broken in that sector, too.

German counterattacks were repelled overnight, and strongpoints were reduced with flamethrowers and explosives, although some hand-to-hand combat occurred. On the evening of the 7th, Hitler sent a communique to Lasch instructing the defenders to fight to the last man. The following day, Vasilevsky appealed to the Germans to surrender, and a futile attempted to break out of the besieged city was repulsed. Finally, Lasch defied Hitler's order as German unit cohesion faltered and initiated surrender discussions that concluded just before midnight on April 9.

Ater the war, the Soviet Union absorbed former East Prussian territory that included Königsberg and renamed the city Kaliningrad.

Soviet soldiers sprint forward during urban combat in the East Prussian capital city of Königsberg. (Government of the Russian Federation via Wikimedia Commons)

German refugees crowd aboard a ship as they attempt to flee Königsberg in early 1945. (Creative Commons Bundesarchiv Bild via Wikimedia Commons)

ANTI-NAZI DIETRICH BONHOEFFER EXECUTED

Dietrich Bonhoeffer, prominent anti-Nazi, poses with a group of children during a church retreat. (Creative Commons Bundesarchiv Bild via Wikimedia Commons)

An early outspoken critic of Adolf Hitler and the Nazi regime, Protestant clergyman Dietrich Bonhoeffer was hanged at Flossenbürg concentration camp in Bavaria along with other prominent leaders of the anti-Nazi resistance just two weeks before the camp's liberation by US Army troops.

Originally a Lutheran pastor, Bonhoeffer was a prominent theologian prior to the rise of the Nazis. His writings on Christian theology and the church in modern times remain widely read, and several of his works are considered classics, particularly the 1937 book *The Cost of Discipleship*.

Bonhoeffer denounced the Nazi persecution of Jews and other minorities in the 1930s and became a founder of the Confessing Church while opposing the infamous Nazi euthanasia programme. While travelling abroad extensively, he described the brutality of the Nazis around the world and even confronted Nazi diplomats he encountered in foreign cities. After serving as pastor of a London church from 1933 to 1935, he returned to Germany and began training new clergy at an underground seminary. By 1938, a Gestapo order had banned him from the German capital of Berlin, and in September 1940 he was forbidden to speak publicly throughout the Third Reich.

As World War Two approached in the late 1930s, Bonhoeffer became aware of numerous resistance groups then active in Germany. His brother-in-law Hans von Dohnanyi assisted him in avoiding military service and helped Bonhoeffer obtain a post in the Reich Intelligence Service, the Abwehr. Continuing to travel abroad from 1941 to 1942, he served as a courier for the resistance.

The first mass deportations of Jews from Berlin began in the autumn of 1941, and Bonhoeffer documented the rounding up and mass movements to the concentration camps along with a fellow member of the Confessing Church who worked as an attorney. A detailed memorandum was prepared and distributed to foreign diplomats in Germany, as well as to individuals in the German military whom they trusted and believed were sympathetic to their cause. Bonhoeffer then became peripherally involved with Operation Seven, a clandestine programme that assisted Jews in escaping from the clutches of the Nazi authorities. Operation Seven issued false papers to escapees that identified them as members of the foreign service.

Bonhoeffer became aware of several plots to assassinate Hitler, but was not actively involved. His association with Operation Seven led to his arrest in April 1943. He was held at Tegel Prison in Berlin for 18 months. In the wake of the failed attempt on Hitler's life on July 20, 1944, Bonhoeffer was implicated due to his ties to several anti-Nazi conspirators. He was transferred to Buchenwald in February 1945 and then executed along with five others, including former Abwehr chief Admiral Wilhelm Canaris.

Left: Clergyman Dietrich Bonhoeffer was an outspoken critic of the Nazi regime and was executed on April 9, 1945. (Creative Commons Bundesarchiv Bild via Wikimedia Commons)

Far left: Former Abwehr chief Admiral Wilhelm Canaris was executed at Flossenbürg concentration camp along with Dietrich Bonhoeffer. (Creative Commons Bundesarchiv Bild via Wikimedia Commons)

KAMIKAZE ATTACKS OFF OKINAWA CONTINUE

At 2.43pm, the battleship USS *Missouri* was on station in the waters near the embattled island of Okinawa. In a flash, a Japanese Mitsubishi A6M Zero fighter struck the starboard side of the ship just below the main deck. The collision sprayed wreckage and aviation fuel across the deck, starting fires. Damage was superficial and the battleship remained on station. The body of the Japanese suicide pilot was recovered and later buried at sea with military honours.

Crews of Kamikazes – translated as Divine Wind in reference to a typhoon that destroyed a Mongol fleet and saved Japan from invasion in the 13th century – wreaked havoc on the US fleet off Okinawa for six days, and attacks on April 11, 1945, were typical of their fury.

Later in the afternoon, the destroyer USS *Kidd* maintained her position on the early warning 'picket line', where advance notice of incoming Japanese suicide attacks was critical in the Fifth Fleet's defence against the menace. After participating in the repulse of three Kamikaze raids along with the destroyers *Black, Chauncey* and *Bullard*, and the brisk intervention of navy fighters flying combat air patrols, *Kidd* was found by a Japanese suicide pilot, who crashed into the ship, killing 38 sailors while wounding 55.

A Kamikaze pilot bears down on the destroyer USS *Kidd* off Okinawa. This photo was taken moments before the aircraft crashed into the American ship, April 11, 1945. (US Navy via Wikimedia Commons)

Kidd fought off further attacks and limped to the forward base at Ulithi for repairs. Meanwhile, the aircraft carrier USS *Enterprise* also took a hit from a Kamikaze and retired temporarily to Ulithi before returning to Okinawan waters. Through the course of the Pacific War, *Enterprise* was attacked by Japanese suicide aircraft six times, taking 13 hits or near-misses.

Altogether on April 11, 1945, six ships of the Fifth Fleet were damaged by Japanese Kamikaze attacks. In desperation, the idea of the suicide pilot willing to give his life for the emperor had been put into practice months earlier during the October 1944 Battle of Leyte Gulf, but at Okinawa the practice reached its zenith.

To oppose the American landings at Okinawa, Admiral Matome Ugaki organised a series of ten Kikusui, or 'Floating Chrysanthemum' mass attacks aimed at the fleet offshore. His Kamikazes flew primarily from airfields on the southern home island of Kyushu, and from April 6 to June 22, 1945, they flew 1,465 missions against the US Navy off Okinawa. Casualties were heavy; 4,907 American sailors were killed or

A Japanese Kamikaze is visible at upper left in this photo, seconds before slamming into the starboard side of the battleship USS *Missouri* off Okinawa, April 11, 1945. (US Navy via Wikimedia Commons)

missing while 29 US Navy ships were sunk and 120 damaged. In turn, 2,373 Kamikaze pilots died in combat.

Later in April, the situation became so critical that Admiral Chester W Nimitz, Commander-in-Chief, Pacific, flew to Okinawa to spur General Simon Bolivar Buckner Jr, to increase the pace of the land campaign. Although withdrawal of the naval force was contemplated, the support force remained in the troubled waters and earned the nickname, "the fleet that came to stay".

The aircraft carrier USS *Enterprise* transfers wounded to the hospital ship *Bountiful* after taking a Kamikaze hit off Okinawa. (US Navy via Wikimedia Commons)

PRESIDENT ROOSEVELT DIES

At 3.32pm, US President Franklin D Roosevelt died at the age of 63 of a cerebral haemorrhage at his cottage nicknamed the Little White House, in Warm Springs, Georgia.

His health visibly failing for some time, Roosevelt had only weeks earlier undertaken his fourth term as president of the United States. Since then, he had travelled extensively, engaging with British Prime Minister Winston Churchill and Soviet Premier Josef Stalin at the Yalta Conference, halfway around the world in the Crimea.

The Yalta trip exhausted the president, and four days of rest at his home in Hyde Park, New York, did not produce the desired return of vigour. Therefore, 'FDR' and his entourage of close friends and relatives travelled to Warm Springs, the train pulling out of Union Station in Washington DC on the afternoon of March 29, 1945.

A heavy smoker his entire adult life, Roosevelt had been diagnosed within the past year with high blood pressure, coronary arterial disease, an enlarged heart and congestive heart failure. Dr Frank Lahey, who had recently examined FDR, noted that he did not believe that if elected to an unprecedented fourth term that the president had the physical capacity to finish it. Lahey further advised Roosevelt to choose carefully his vice-presidential running mate for that very reason.

The morning of April 12 began as usual. FDR read a backlog of newspapers and then turned his

Visibly frail, President Roosevelt confers with King Ibn Saud of Saudi Arabia just after the conclusion of the Yalta Conference. (US Army Signal Corps via Wikimedia Commons)

attention to a large volume of mail. He signed official documents, setting them aside for the ink from his fountain pen to dry, and chuckled at his own joke that the small office resembled a laundry with papers laid about.

Afterwards, the president sat for artist Elizabeth Shoumatoff, who was painting his portrait. The butler began setting the table for lunch at 1pm, and FDR smiled, saying: "We've got just 15 minutes more." The artist remembered that he was in fine spirits and took note of his good skin colour. She also recalled a sudden change. "He raised his right hand and passed it over his forehead several times in a strange jerky way… He looked at me, his forehead furrowed with pain, and tried to smile. He put his left hand up to the back of his head and said, 'I have a terrific pain in the back of my head' and then he collapsed."

A doctor was summoned and concluded that the president had suffered a cerebral haemorrhage. FDR's heavy, laboured breathing was heard from room to room. Eleanor Roosevelt, who had remained in Washington, was notified that her husband had become ill and received word of his death later in the afternoon. She cabled her adult children: "Father slept away. He would expect you to carry on and finish your jobs."

News of Roosevelt's death spread across the globe, and tributes poured in to the capital city. Prime Minister Churchill told the House of Commons: "For us, it remains only to say that in Franklin Roosevelt there died the greatest American friend we have ever known, and the greatest champion of freedom who has ever brought help and comfort from the New World to the Old."

Mourners lined the 700-mile route of the president's funeral train from Warm Springs to Washington. A private funeral was held in the East Room of the White House, and final burial took place in the rose garden at Hyde Park, New York, on April 15.

After being sworn in as the 33rd President of the United States, Harry Truman asked Eleanor if there was anything he could do for the family. She responded: "Is there anything that we can do for you. You are the one in trouble now."

Left: Taken the day before his death, this last photograph of President Roosevelt was intended for artist Elizabeth Shoumatoff. (Franklin D Roosevelt Presidential Library and Museum via Wikimedia Commons)

Below: The horse-drawn caisson carrying President Roosevelt's coffin proceeds down Pennsylvania Avenue in Washington DC. (Library of Congress Print and Photograph Division via Wikimedia Commons)

BRITISH FORCES LIBERATE BERGEN-BELSEN

After Nazi Reichsführer SS Heinrich Himmler agreed to relinquish control without a fight and established a 19-mile exclusion zone to prevent the spread of typhus, British forces liberated the infamous concentration camp of Bergen-Belsen in Lower Saxony. The first Allied soldier to come upon the camp was Lieutenant John Randall of the Special Air Service, while on a reconnaissance mission. Within hours the British 11th Armoured Division had arrived in force, and the troops were taken aback at the ghastly sight.

The liberators found about 50,000 inmates, all of them suffering from starvation and a variety of diseases, including typhus, typhoid fever, dysentery and tuberculosis. Many were seriously ill and too weak to comprehend that their deliverance was at hand. The prisoners had been deprived of food and water for days, and approximately 13,000 corpses lay unburied and scattered across the camp. Immediately, the liberators began to distribute humanitarian aid, while some inmates turned on their former guards to exact revenge. Dozens of collaborators were beaten to death.

BBC Correspondent Richard Dimbleby witnessed the grim scene and later commented: "Here over an acre of ground lay dead and dying people. You could not see which was which… The living lay with their heads against the corpses and around them moved the awful, ghostly procession of emaciated, aimless people, with nothing to do and with no hope of life, unable to move out of your way, unable to look at the terrible sights around them."

Bergen-Belsen was originally constructed as a military camp by the German Army in 1935. With the outbreak of World War Two in 1939, it became a prisoner of

Former Bergen-Belsen guards are forced to load corpses onto a truck for transportation to a mass grave. (Collections of the Imperial War Museums via Wikimedia Commons)

A British soldier watches former Bergen-Belsen camp guard Irma Grese and commandant Josef Kramer, known as the 'Beast of Belsen'. (Collections of the Imperial War Museums via Wikimedia Commons)

war camp, where as many as 95,000 POWs were held by the following year. After the June 22, 1941, Nazi invasion of the Soviet Union, thousands of Red Army prisoners were held at Bergen-Belsen, and after the camp's liberation nearly 20,000 graves of Soviet military personnel were counted. In April 1943, the SS took control of a portion of the expanded complex, and over the following 18 months several thousand Jews were transported there.

After the liberation, the death rate remained as high as 500 per day. However, within a month nearly 30,000 former inmates were relocated to displaced persons camps. The British ordered the former SS guards and administrative personnel to bury the dead, and photographs were taken depicting the use of bulldozers to fill mass graves. Bergen-Belsen was subsequently burned to the ground to eliminate a massive lice infestation and quell the typhus epidemic.

From 1941 to 1945, an estimated 70,000 people died in Bergen-Belsen; the most famous of these was Anne Frank, the young girl whose diary captivated the world. She succumbed to typhus, as did her sister, Margot, in February or March 1945. Her father, Otto, was the only surviving member of the family.

In the autumn of 1945, the British Military tribunal at Lüneburg placed 48 former Bergen-Belsen officers and workers on trial for war crimes. Among them was ex-commandant Josef Kramer. He was found guilty and sentenced to death by hanging along with 11 others. Nineteen defendants received lengthy prison terms; 14 individuals were acquitted. The death sentences were carried out on December 12, 1945.

This view of the sprawling camp at Bergen-Belsen was taken shortly after its liberation. (Collections of the Imperial War Museums via Wikimedia Commons)

FAMED CORRESPONDENT ERNIE PYLE KILLED

Although thousands of US military personnel were killed or wounded during the fight for Okinawa and neighbouring islands in the Ryukyus group, perhaps the most famous of those lost is beloved war correspondent Ernie Pyle, a non-combatant.

Pyle was accompanying the troops of the 77th Infantry Division in their mission to secure the tiny spit of land called Ie Shima. The correspondent – whose syndicated column was published in 700 newspapers across the United States – was riding in a Jeep with four others when a Japanese machine gun barked. The occupants took cover in a ditch, and Pyle inadvertently raised his head. A single machine-gun or rifle bullet struck his temple and he died instantly.

Pyle was widely known and admired by the American public and also the men in uniform. His candid, personal style conveyed the experiences of the ordinary soldier, in the muddy foxholes, dashing through enemy fire, celebrating survival and mourning the loss of a friend on the battlefield. He talked to the men, got to know them in the desert of North Africa, the rugged mountains of Italy, and then journeyed to the Pacific. He received a 1944 Pulitzer Prize for his crisp, unvarnished accounts of men at war. His wartime books, *Here Is Your War*, published in 1943, and *Brave Men*, released the next year, remain classics of wartime storytelling, and he was portrayed by actor Burgess Meredith in the wartime film *The Story of GI Joe*.

Pyle had come ashore on Okinawa on Love Day, April 1, 1945. Along with the US Marines and Army troops he accompanied, the lack of opposition astonished him: "Never before had I seen an invasion beach like Okinawa," he wrote. "There wasn't a dead or wounded man in our whole sector of it. Medical corpsmen were sitting among their sacks of bandages and plasma with nothing to do. There wasn't a single burning vehicle, nor a single boat lying wrecked on the reef or shoreline. The carnage that is almost inevitable on an invasion was wonderfully and beautifully not there."

This moment of relief was all too short. The situation changed as the Americans moved inland, and Pyle went with them. He decided to

Ernie Pyle talks with a tank crew from the 191st Tank Battalion in Italy, 1944. (US Army via Wikimedia Commons)

tag along with the 77th to observe them in action at Ie Shima, where an airfield had to be taken and 5,000 Japanese soldiers either killed or captured. The fight for the islet took six days and cost the 77th Division 1,100 casualties.

Pyle was buried near where he fell, still wearing his helmet. His body was later exhumed and interred at the National Memorial Cemetery of the Pacific, on the island of Oahu, Hawaii. A stone tablet stands where he was killed and reads: "At this spot, the 77th Infantry lost a buddy, Ernie Pyle, 18 April 1945."

President Harry Truman remarked: "More than any other man, he became the spokesman of the ordinary American-in-arms doing so many extraordinary things." Pyle was one of the few civilians in American military history to be awarded the Purple Heart medal.

Above: Famed war correspondent Ernie Pyle was killed by a Japanese bullet on the islet of Ie Shima. (Library of Congress Photographs and Prints Division via Wikimedia Commons)

Left: American troops gather for the funeral of Ernie Pyle shortly after he was killed on Ie Shima. (US Navy via Wikimedia Commons)

HITLER'S 56TH BIRTHDAY IN THE FÜHRERBUNKER

SS troops march stiffly down the Unter den Linden in Berlin during Hitler's 50th birthday celebration in 1939. (Creative Commons Bundesarchiv Bild via Wikimedia Commons)

Adolf Hitler, his dream of a 'Thousand Year Reich' collapsing around him, observed his 56th birthday, spending much of the day in the dank confines of the Führerbunker, buried 50ft below ground in the garden of the Reich Chancellery in the Nazi capital of Berlin.

The Führer, once robust, exuding confidence and filled with National Socialist fervour, was a mere shadow of his former self. His hands trembled with the progression of Parkinson's Disease. He slumped noticeably and shuffled as he walked. His eyes were glassy and hollow, and a chemical cocktail of Benzedrine and eye drops laced with cocaine allowed him to function during the day; only barbiturates could induce some fitful sleep. He suffered from constant stomach pain.

Once vibrant, the Führer's physical and mental state hovered in the gloaming of catatonic dejection, emotional hysteria and blind rage. Worse still, the Allies were closing in on the heart of Nazi Germany. Soviet spearheads were poised to begin their direct assault on Berlin. Trust in the members of his inner circle had begun to erode, and there was little prospect for a reversal of fortune save the fantasies that sometimes caused Hitler to issue orders to Wehrmacht units incapable of executing the directives or that had already been consumed in the conflagration of war and now existed only in his addled mind.

On this day, Hitler's personal secretary Martin Bormann noted in his personal diary: "Führer's birthday but unfortunately no mood for celebration."

During the afternoon, Hitler emerged from the relative safety of the Führerbunker for a brief period. His purpose was to present the Iron Cross for valour in the fight against the approaching Red Army to a group of young soldiers, the eldest of whom was probably no more than 15 years old. Hitler was nearly swallowed up in an ill-fitting greatcoat as he walked past the line of devoted youth, some of whom

A haggard Adolf Hitler presents the Iron Cross to a youthful German soldier on April 20, 1945, the Führer's 56th birthday. (Unknown Author Public Domain European Union via Wikimedia Commons)

In this photo, believed to have been taken in March 1945, Hitler discusses the deteriorating military situation with a group of his generals. (Creative Commons Bundesarchiv Bild via Wikimedia Common)

This photograph was taken by Hitler's personal photographer, Heinrich Hoffmann, during the Führer's last public appearance on April 20, 1945, his 56th birthday. (Creative Commons Public Domain Popperfoto/Getty Images via Wikimedia Commons)

Luftwaffe aircraft fly in formation above a crowd gathered to celebrate Hitler's 50th birthday. The situation had changed markedly six years later. (Creative Commons Rijksmuseum via Wikimedia Commons)

would no doubt die in the rubble of Berlin in the coming days. He managed a slight smile at times, stopping to pinch and pat the cheek of one of the Iron Cross recipients. The Führer was physically unable to present the medals to the recipients as his hands were too unsteady. His left arm convulses uncontrollably in the grainy film of the event, and he keeps it tightly clenched behind his back.

Hitler returned to the Führerbunker later in the afternoon and received several of his closest associates, including Reichsführer SS Heinrich Himmler, Propaganda Minister Josef Goebbels and Luftwaffe chief Hermann Göring. They expressed obligatory good wishes for the occasion, but the atmosphere was sombre. The event was in stark contrast to the grandeur and spectacle of the Nazi leader's 50th birthday in 1939. Just six years earlier the Führer had basked in the ascendancy of the Nazi regime after several diplomatic victories had led to bloodless territorial gains and the terms of the odious Versailles Treaty had been repudiated as the German military unveiled its resurrected might to the world.

In 1939, a massive military parade had included 50,000 soldiers, while 162 Luftwaffe aircraft flew overhead in salute and thousands of spectators lined the streets of Berlin. At night, the Unter den Linden and other major thoroughfares in the capital city, festooned with Swastika banners, had been lit up, monuments decorated and Nazi flags fluttered from the Brandenburg Gate. But in 1945 those moments were only a fleeting memory as retribution was at hand.

Those residents of the Führerbunker who survived to tell tales of the Nazi twilight remembered that Hitler had preferred that no formal birthday observance should be held on April 20, 1945. Nevertheless, a few bottles of champagne were brought out, and food was prepared for the gloomy gathering that took on the look and feel of a funeral wake. The Führer acknowledged the effort and then excused himself, leaving the group, including his longtime companion Eva Braun, to observe the occasion without the guest of honour.

The whine of the ventilation system was pervasive throughout the massive subterranean bunker, providing an eerie essence of doom in the background. Still, the champagne was consumed while the would-be celebrants talked of better days and reminisced. A single record is available for the gramophone, and *Blutrote Rosen (Blood Red Roses)* played continually. Famed tenor Max Mensing, who took his own life with poison in Berlin during the last days of the war, had popularised the tune in the late 1920s.

The stilted revelry proceeded as some tried to dance. Ripples of laughter were punctuated with periods of awkward silence and the conversation drifted. Traudl Junge, one of Hitler's secretaries, could scarcely bear to watch the macabre celebration: "It was horrible; soon I couldn't stand it and went back down to bed," she wrote in her diary.

As bizarre as the day had been, worse was yet to come. In smoke and flame, the Thousand Year Reich would soon crumble.

Twelve-year-old Alfred Czech was one of the boys who received the Iron Cross from Hitler on April 20, 1945. (Creative Commons Bundesarchiv Bild via Wikimedia Commons)

BATTLE OF BERLIN BEGINS

As Soviet artillery continually pounded Berlin, the Red Army initiated the final assault on the Nazi capital. For nearly two years, the inexorable Russian tide had pushed the Germans back steadily westward more than 1,000 miles. Since the Nazi invasion of the Soviet Union on June 22, 1941, the two nations had been locked in a death struggle. Now, two Red Army Fronts – the 1st Belorussian under Marshal Georgi Zhukov and the 1st Ukrainian under Marshal Ivan Konev – 2.5 million men, seeking vengeance against the hated Nazi enemy, assaulted the city.

Two weeks earlier, Soviet Premier Josef Stalin had summoned Zhukov and Konev to the Kremlin in Moscow and posed the question: "Who will take Berlin?" Konev declared: "We will!" Stalin then issued the orders initiating a competition between the two. Zhukov was to attack Berlin from the north and east while Konev approached from the south. The two massive forces would converge in a great pincer, surrounding the city and reducing resistance in an ever-tightening perimeter.

Konev gained ground steadily in the advance to Berlin, but Zhukov encountered stiff resistance in several locations, including Seelöw Heights about 50 miles from the capital. Stalin flew into a rage and ordered the combined effort redoubled. Konev was told to abandon his wide swing and to send his armoured spearheads directly into the city as soon as possible. When the Red Army closed to within range of field artillery, more guns thundered. A news correspondent remembered the moment the guns began their intense barrage on April 22. He wrote: "'What are the targets?' I asked the battery commander. 'Centre of Berlin, Spree bridges and the northern Stettin railway stations,' he answered. Then came the tremendous words of command, 'Open fire on the capital of Fascist Germany!'"

The Germans had divided Berlin's defences into three concentric circles, the outermost stretching 60 miles around the outskirts of the city and consisting mostly of thinly-held roadblocks, heaps of rubble and shallow trenches. The second circle ran 25 miles and encompassed the S-Bahn, Berlin's public railway transportation system. The inner ring included large buildings that were formerly occupied by ministries and government offices, now transformed into strongpoints bristling with machine guns, each floor to be defended. Six massive concrete flak towers were incorporated, virtually impervious to anything short of a

The rubble and desolation of this Berlin street just off the Unter den Linden bears witness to the ferocity of the battle for the Nazi capital city. (Collections of the Imperial War Museums via Wikimedia Commons)

Soviet artillery batters Berlin during the Red Army drive to capture the Nazi capital city, April 1945.
(Creative Commons Bundesarchiv Bild via Wikimedia Commons)

direct hit. Eight pie-shaped dividing sectors radiated from the centre of Berlin, crossing each ring to the outer perimeter. These were identified A through H; a ninth sector, labelled Z, was defended by fanatical members of Hitler's personal SS bodyguard.

Berlin spanned 340sq miles, and strong defensive positions were built along the Landwehr and Teltow Canals and the River Spree. The main objective of the converging Soviet forces was the cluster of government buildings known as the Citadel, which included the Reichstag and other structures, north and east of the Tiergarten, a large park and residential district that included the Berlin Zoo.

The strength of Berlin's defenders, estimated between 100,000 and 180,000, included SS and Wehrmacht troops and the old men and boys of the Volkssturm and Hitler Youth. These were under the command of General Helmuth Weidling.

The Soviets breached the first defence line with relative ease and had fought their way through the second by April 26. They crossed the S-Bahn line and assaulted Tempelhof Airport. In the west, Zhukov's troops entered Charlottenburg and reached the Spree. Two days later, the Potsdamerstrasse Bridge across the Landwehr Canal was captured and the fighting reached the Tiergarten.

At the end of the month, the 79th Rifle Corps undertook a concerted effort to capture the Reichstag by direct assault. Troops of the 150th Rifle Division sprinted across the Konigsplatz directly in front of the building and attacked both flanks, too. Three assaults were thrown back between 4.30am and 1pm. The 128mm guns atop the flak tower near the Berlin Zoo took a toll on the attackers, firing from more than a mile away. At 6pm, the 14-hour fight for the Reichstag was renewed. The entries were breached and fighting inside the building was hand-to-hand and floor-by-floor.

the 8th Guards Army – requesting another meeting. Weidling was instructed to proceed to the Potsdamerstrasse Bridge. He was then taken to Chuikov's headquarters, and after talks were concluded, Weidling issued orders for the defenders to lay down their arms. Some pockets of fanatical resistance remained, but the fight for the Nazi capital was over.

The cost had been tremendous. Soviet losses were estimated at 350,000 killed, wounded or captured, while the Germans suffered 450,000 military casualties with an estimated 300,000 civilians dead or wounded.

The heavily damaged Reichstag building in Berlin is shown after its capture by Red Army troops. (Collections of the Imperial War Museums via Wikimedia Commons)

A Soviet soldier raises the Red Banner atop the Reichstag in Berlin. (Yevgeny Khaldei Tass via Wikimedia Commons)

The iconic Brandenburg Gate bears the scars of battle after the Soviets took control of the city. (Creative Commons Bundesarchiv Bild via Wikimedia Commons)

Two soldiers found a stairway to the roof and jammed the Red Hammer and Sickle banner of the Soviet Union into a cleft in an equestrian statue atop the building. However, diehard defenders of the Reichstag held out until May 2. After the building was declared secure, the placing of the Red Banner was re-enacted for a camera crew and famous photos of the event were taken during the staged production.

On the morning of April 30, General Weidling had informed Hitler that the Soviets would control the centre of Berlin within hours. That afternoon, Hitler and his wife, Eva Braun Hitler, committed suicide in the Führerbunker, beneath the rose garden of the Reich Chancellery. At the same time, elements of the Soviet 5th Shock, 8th Guards and 8th Guards Tank Armies advanced down the Unter den Linden toward the Reich Chancellery as only about 10,000 Germans remained active in defence. Soviet tanks and self-propelled guns pounded the Air Ministry building and the heart of Berlin was cut in half in the movement.

After initial entreaties for surrender terms broke down on May 1, General Weidling contacted General Vasily Chuikov – commanding

Pressed into service, German soldiers of the Volkssturm carry shoulder-fired Panzerfaust anti-tank weapons. (Creative Commons Bundesarchiv Bild via Wikimedia Commons)

LUFTWAFFE CHIEF GÖRING MAKES POWER BID

While Berlin languished in smoke and flame and Adolf Hitler and his entourage endured the nightmare of the Führerbunker, Luftwaffe chief Reichsmarschall Hermann Göring retreated to the relative safety of Berchtesgaden in the Bavarian Alps. Sensing an opportunity to exercise greater authority, even as the Third Reich was crumbling, Göring issued an electrifying communiqué that reverberated throughout the Nazi hierarchy.

Launching a bid for power in the dire circumstances, Göring declared: "My Führer, General Koller today gave me a briefing on the basis of communications given to him by Colonel General Jodl and General Christian, according to which you had referred certain decisions to me and emphasised that I, in case negotiations would become necessary, would be in an easier position than you in Berlin. These views were so surprising and serious to me that I felt obligated to assume, in case by 2200 o'clock no answer is forthcoming, that you have lost your freedom of action. I shall then view the conditions of your decree as fulfilled and take action for the well-being of Nation and Fatherland. You know what I feel for you in these most difficult hours of my life and I cannot express this in words. God

Hermann Göring, third from left, stands with Hitler, Martin Bormann and Hitler Youth Leader Baldur von Schirach at Berchtesgaden in the Bavarian Alps. (Creative Commons Bundesarchiv Bild via Wikimedia Commons)

protect you and allow you despite everything to come here as soon as possible. Your faithful Hermann Göring."

Martin Bormann, Hitler's personal secretary, stalked into the Führer's presence to deliver the message. The response was predictable. Hitler flew into a rage, screaming for Göring's arrest. He summarily stripped Göring of all ranks and titles and immediately dictated a terse response that the former deputy führer has committed high treason. Hitler saw Göring's action as treacherous, the highest form of treason. The cruellest blow was the apparent fact that even his closest associates were falling away.

Reich Minister of Armaments Albert Speer, perhaps Hitler's only 'real' friend, wrote in his landmark book, *Inside The Third Reich,* that the moment was "…an outburst of wild fury… in which feelings of bitterness, helplessness, self-pity and despair mingled".

A short time later, insult was heaped on injury when British news reports noted that Reichsführer Heinrich Himmler, whom Hitler called "Faithful Heinrich", had been conducting separate and unauthorised peace talks with the Allies through Swedish diplomatic channels. Hitler condemned Himmler, ordering his immediate arrest, and in reprisal had SS General Hermann Fegelein, Himmler's liaison in the Führerbunker and Eva Braun's brother-in-law, summarily shot.

In happier days, Hermann Göring stands before the Führer who delivers a stiff Nazi salute. (National Archives and Records Administration via Wikimedia Commons)

Once most highly favoured in the Nazi hierarchy, Hermann Göring shares the adoration of a crowd from a balcony of the Reich Chancellery. (Creative Commons Bundesarchiv Bild via Wikimedia Commons)

US, SOVIET FORCES LINK UP AT TORGAU

An American and Soviet soldier embrace after linking up at Torgau on the River Elbe.
(National Archives and Records Administration via Wikimedia Commons)

Allied armies would concentrate on clearing the industrialised Ruhr, frustrating General William Simpson, whose Ninth Army was about 90 miles from Berlin on reaching the Elbe.

Eisenhower's decision was based on the logic that Soviet spearheads had already crossed the River Oder in mid-March and were well on their way to Berlin. Further, many soldiers were destined to fight and die in the major battle while diplomats were working out details of a post-war occupation of the city that would require its division into four zones administered by the Soviet Union, United States, Great Britain and France. Therefore, even if American troops captured the Nazi capital, they would be required to relinquish control of much of the city.

Eisenhower partially acted on the advice he received from West Point classmate and long-time friend General Omar Bradley, commander of the Allied 12th Army Group, while the two rested a few days at the resort town of Cannes on the French Riviera. Bradley had commented that an estimated 100,000 American casualties would be "a pretty stiff price to pay for a prestige objective, especially when we've got to fall back and let the other fellow take over".

From the Mulde line, Lieutenant Albert Kotzebue led a 35-man patrol from the 273rd Regiment, 69th Infantry Division towards the west bank of the Elbe on April 25, 1945. Although a prearranged recognition signal of green flares had been agreed on by the converging Allied troops, the first recognition was likely to be by sight. The Americans probed within a mile of the river, and witnesses reported the sighting of a lone Red Army soldier riding a horse.

Lt Kotzebue rowed across the Elbe and established contact with soldiers of the Soviet 58th Guards Rifle Division, 5th Guards Army. Handshakes East and West took place on a damaged bridge across the waterway. The soldiers embraced, celebrated with music and toasts, and exchanged souvenirs. Nazi Germany was split in two.

Left: Stretching across the bridge over the Elbe that has been partially destroyed by the Germans, US and Soviet soldiers shake hands. (Creative Commons Aagnverglaser via Wikimedia Commons)

Below: American and Soviet soldiers celebrate their link-up at the River Elbe on April 25, 1945. (Russian Federation Public Domain via Wikimedia Commons)

The US First Army was steadily advancing into Germany and on April 24 its vanguard reached the line of the River Mulde in the province of Saxony. The following day, patrols were extended eastwards with the prospect of the first contact between American combat troops and their counterparts in the Soviet Red Army in Europe. A day later, American and Soviet soldiers shook hands at the town of Torgau on the River Elbe.

General Dwight D Eisenhower, Supreme Commander of Allied Forces in Western Europe, held firm in his decision that the capture of Berlin – the Nazi capital – should be left to the Soviets and ordered the forces in the centre of the Allied broad front to advance no further than the Elbe. Concerns surrounding the possibility of a friendly fire incident prompted him to modify his orders to the First Army to halt at the Mulde, some distance to the west.

Eisenhower had circumvented the chain of command previously, bypassing diplomatic channels and sending direct assurances to Soviet Premier Josef Stalin that the capture of Berlin would be left to the Red Army. The Western

MUSSOLINI EXECUTED

As the last days of World War Two in Italy played out, deposed Fascist dictator Benito Mussolini and his mistress, 33-year-old Clara Petacci, were executed by Communist partisans near the town of Dongo. The death of 'Il Duce', once adored by the Italian people, ended a bizarre series of events that had seen him rise to the heights of power, partner with Nazi Germany and Imperial Japan in the Axis, engage in ill-advised military operations and then fall from power.

In 1943, as Allied forces fought for control of Italian soil on the island of Sicily, Mussolini had been ousted from office by a vote of his once loyal Fascist Grand Council. Arrested and imprisoned, the dictator was helpless as the Italian government led by newly appointed Prime Minister Pietro Badoglio switched sides and joined the Allies. Mussolini was rescued in a daring German airborne and commando operation led by SS Major Otto Skorzeny, plucked from the Hotel Campo Imperatore on the heights of the Gran Sasso in the Appenine Mountains. He was spirited to safety, meeting briefly with his benefactor Adolf Hitler in Munich and then being installed as head of the Nazi-inspired Italian Socialist Republic.

By the spring of 1945, the military situation in Italy was rapidly deteriorating as the Germans and the few diehard Fascists who fought alongside them were pushed northward. On April 25, Mussolini and Petacci left the city of Milan, their destination the town of Como in Lombardy, northern Italy, where they believed they would rendezvous with a force of 3,000 or more loyal Fascists who intended to continue the fight. Il Duce would then lead these men into the mountains

Above: The battered bodies of Mussolini, Clara Petacci and other Fascists hang in the Piazzale Loreto. (Government of Italy Public Domain via Wikimedia Commons)

Right: Clara Petacci, mistress of Benito Mussolini, was executed with Il Duce on April 28, 1945. (Government of Italy Public Domain via Wikimedia Commons)

to carry on a spirited campaign from their alpine redoubt. However, Mussolini came face to face with the grim reality of the situation as only 12 soldiers responded to the rallying effort.

With no alternative, the small band of Fascists sought refuge with a German convoy headed northwards. Mussolini realised that he was a hunted man in his own country and dressed in an oversize German greatcoat and a helmet to partially cover his face in the hopes of concealing his identity. As the convoy approached Dongo the following day, it was halted by Communist partisans under the command of Count Pierluigi Bellini delle Stelle. For a while it appeared that Mussolini's ruse might save him from capture. But one of the partisan fighters noticed that the leather boots this 'German soldier' was wearing were actually of exceptionally high quality. Further investigation revealed the identity of Il Duce and his mistress.

Mussolini and Petacci were taken into custody at gunpoint, and the prisoners were held under guard for the next two days while the Communist leaders of the Committee for National Liberation deliberated the disposition of this former national hero turned enemy of the state. The events of April 28, 1945, are still surrounded by theory and conjecture, but the most likely scenario leading to the deaths of Mussolini and Petacci is quite plausible.

The prevailing story goes that the guards herded the two onto a truck that waited nearby. The driver is believed to have been a partisan named Walter Audisio. He drove the truck to a villa some distance away and on arrival ordered the passengers to exit and stand beside a low wall. Reports state that Audisio pointed a submachine gun and his own pistol at Petacci, but both apparently jammed.

Audisio was then said to have taken a weapon from another partisan named Moretti and shot Petacci to death. He then turned toward the condemned Il Duce. At this point, accounts vary as to the exact circumstances of Mussolini's final moments. Some witnesses claimed that Mussolini was a trembling coward, begging for his life and moaning an offer to his captors: "I will give you an empire!" Others recalled that the condemned man tore open his coat and shirt with a flourish, baring his barrel chest, and exclaimed: "Shoot me in the chest!" A burst from the automatic weapon finished the execution, and the former strongman of Fascist Italy crumbled to the ground in a heap.

The bodies were loaded into the back of a yellow furniture truck and driven to the Piazzale Loreto in Milan, where five major roads of northern Italy converged. They were unceremoniously dumped there at approximately 3am, on Sunday April 29. Sixteen other bodies, suspected Fascists and victims of other Communist execution squads, were also deposited there. News of the death of Il Duce circulated swiftly in a special edition of the local newspaper and broadcasts of Radio Free Milan.

A crowd gathered to exact macabre vengeance on the Fascists' corpses. The bodies of Mussolini, Petacci and four others were strung up by the heels like slaughtered animals from a girder in an unfinished petrol station. Amid jeers and taunts, some

Mussolini strikes a defiant pose while leading the Fascist March on Rome in 1922. (Government of Italy Public Domain via Wikimedia Commons)

Mussolini strides past an adoring throng of Fascist youths at a 1935 rally. (European Union Public Domain via Wikimedia Commons)

individuals stepped forward to beat the corpses. Others spat on them. One woman brandished a pistol and emptied it into the lifeless bodies while shouting: "Five shots for my five murdered sons!"

Mussolini's battered remains were soon hastily buried in an unmarked grave, but a year later loyal Fascists exhumed the body and hid it in a convent. Finally, in 1957, Il Duce was laid to rest in his family's crypt in the cemetery of San Cassiano in the Italian town of Predappio.

Left: Both men at the zenith of their power and prestige, Mussolini stands with Hitler at Munich in 1940. (Unknown Author Public Domain via Wikimedia Commons)

Far left: Italian Fascist dictator Benito Mussolini met an ignominious end, executed by Italian Communist partisans. (Government of Italy Public Domain via Wikimedia Commons)

US 45TH DIVISION LIBERATES DACHAU

Dachau, the oldest of the Nazi concentration camps, was liberated by soldiers of the US 45th Infantry Division, while a subcamp a short distance away was also liberated by troops of the 42nd Infantry Division.

When the American troops of the XV Corps under General Wade Haislip approached Dachau, located about ten miles northwest of Munich, senior officers were aware that a ghastly sight might unfold before them. Escapees had told of the atrocities in the death camps, while the liberation of Buchenwald about 220 miles north on April 11 had laid bare the extent of Nazi depravity.

Colonel Kenneth Worthing, 45th Division Planning Officer, prepared action steps for what he believed would be encountered: "We will uncover concentration camp at Dachau, containing unknown number of prisoners (reports vary from 12,000 to 30,000). This camp is the most important concentration camp in Germany and many famous, important persons and much valuable information may be in the camp… Conditions at the camp will probably be bad, insofar as food, health and sanitation are concerned. Prior to our occupation of the camp, the German guards may have left and many of the prisoners may have departed… Danger from typhus and other diseases, and security measures, require that control be exercised over the large number of curiosity seekers who may be expected to flock to the camp."

Despite the effort of Worthing, no individual soldier was prepared for the hellish scene encountered at Dachau. The first hint of what would be uncovered was the sickening odour of decaying flesh, disease and death. The first of the Nazi concentration camps, Dachau was established in 1933 only five weeks after the rise of Hitler's despicable regime to full power in Germany. At first the camp held only about 5,000 political prisoners, but in time it was expanded to hold thousands more – Jews, gypsies, Jehovah's Witnesses, homosexuals, Slavs and other perceived undesirables.

When the American troops reached the gates of Dachau, they found approximately 30,000 emaciated and disease-ridden survivors, while nearly 68,000 people had recently occupied the site. The Germans had evacuated some internees to other camps and about 7,000 Jews had been forced to begin walking far to the south to Tegernsee just two days earlier. Approximately 30 railroad cars were found, filled with decomposing corpses. Soldiers who had been in combat for 500 days or more were overcome by the sight and the stench, retching or breaking down in disbelief. Bodies of the dead and dying were strewn everywhere. One soldier remembered that in places they were "stacked like cordwood".

A handful of Germans, former guards and officers, remained in the vicinity, and when they were located many were immediately shot

US soldiers at the entrance to the infamous Nazi concentration camp at Dachau in the spring of 1945. (National Archives and Records Administration via Wikimedia Commons)

or beaten to death. American soldiers vented their rage, shooting an estimated 30 Germans.

During the course of its odious existence, the Dachau complex is believed to have held 250,000 prisoners. While many were transported to other camps, at least 32,000 people perished at Dachau. In the days after the liberation, the inhabitants of the nearby town of the same name were ordered to assist in the burials of about 9,000 people who had died in such cruel circumstances at the hands of their countrymen.

American soldiers guard German prisoners in a coal yard at the Dachau concentration camp. (National Archives and Records Administration via Wikimedia Commons)

Newly arrived Jewish internees stand in ranks at Dachau in the late 1930s, their fate terribly uncertain. (Creative Commons Bundesarchiv Bild via Wikimedia Commons)

HITLER COMMITS SUICIDE IN THE FÜHRERBUNKER

This image of the exterior of the Führerbunker was taken shortly before the structure was demolished. Today, little evidence of it remains. (Creative Commons Bundesarchiv Bild via Wikimedia Commons)

Finally realising that the dream of the 'Thousand Year Reich' was in ruin, Adolf Hitler, leader of Nazi Germany for only 12 years, committed suicide in the Führerbunker beneath the smoking rubble of Berlin along with his long-time mistress Eva Braun, whom he married only hours earlier. With Hitler dead, the scene in the subterranean bunker unravelled into chaos.

Bits of concrete and dust fell from the ceiling of the Führerbunker as Hitler had received word that Benito Mussolini and his mistress Clara Petacci had been murdered by Communist partisans in Italy. The Führer realised that time was short. He distributed cyanide capsules to those who remained in the bunker and dispelled doubts as to its potency by crushing a capsule between the teeth of Blondi, his beloved Alsatian, given to him as a puppy by personal secretary Martin Bormann in 1941. The dog died instantly.

Just days earlier, Hitler had confided in his Armaments Minister Albert Speer that he had come to grips with the fact that all hope was lost. "That day he said nothing more of an imminent turning point or that there was still hope," Speer wrote in his memoir, *Inside The Third Reich*. "Rather apathetically, wearily and if it were already a matter of course, he began speaking of his death… 'I shall not fight personally. There is always the danger that I would be wounded and fall into the hands of the Russians alive. I don't want my enemies to disgrace my body either. I've given orders that I be cremated. Fraülein Braun wants to depart this life with me… Believe me, Speer, it is easy for me to end my life. A brief moment and I'm freed of everything, liberated from this painful existence.' I felt as if I had been talking to a man already

Right: SS officer Heinz Linge, Hitler's valet, was one of the first individuals to view the body of the dead Führer. (Creative Commons Bundesarchiv Bild via Wikimedia Commons)

Below: Days before his death by suicide, Adolf Hitler visits soldiers sworn to defend Berlin to the last. (Creative Commons Bundesarchiv Bild via Wikimedia Commons)

During a July 1945 visit to war-ravaged Berlin, Prime Minister Winston Churchill sits in a chair taken from the Führerbunker. (Collections of the Imperial War Museums via Wikimedia Commons)

on his head. I saw Eva with her knees drawn up lying next to him on the sofa…" Hitler was dead from a single bullet wound to the temple and had apparently crushed a cyanide capsule in his teeth while pulling the trigger. Eva had died quickly from cyanide poisoning.

SS officer Erich Kempka, the Führer's chauffeur, returned soon after a foray to gather 170 litres of petrol to douse the bodies and ignite a blazing pyre. Ludwig Stumpfegger, one of Hitler's doctors, assisted Linge in carrying the Führer's lifeless body up the long stairs and into the garden of the Reich Chancellery. Bormann followed with Eva's corpse slung over his shoulder.

Soviet artillery rounds fell nearby, making the duty hazardous, so the cremation detail worked quickly. The bodies were deposited in a shallow grave conveniently formed by an artillery shell's impact. Kempka, Linge and SS officer Otto Günsche, Hitler's personal adjutant, emptied the numerous cans of petrol on the bodies of their dead leader and his wife. Linge found a rag and set it alight, then tossed it into the grave. In a flash, the bodies were blazing.

Soon after the suicides, the inhabitants of the Führerbunker took different paths to their own ignominious ends. With the surrender of Berlin just hours later, Soviet soldiers discovered the charred bodies of Hitler and Eva Braun.

departed. The atmosphere grew rapidly uncanny: the tragedy was nearing its end."

Late in the evening of April 29, Hitler dictated his last will and testament to secretary Traudl Junge. He ranted against the perceived worldwide Jewish-Bolshevik conspiracy: "It is untrue that I or anyone else in Germany wanted war in 1939. It was desired and instigated exclusively by those… statesmen who were either of Jewish descent or worked for Jewish interests." A final administrative act appointed Kriegsmarine Admiral Karl Dönitz as his successor to lead in the last days of the Third Reich.

A local Reich official was summoned to join Hitler and Braun in marriage, a surreal event considering the surroundings. There was little celebration, and the denizens of the Führerbunker began to smoke and drink alcohol freely despite the fact that Hitler detested both. They talked about preferred methods of suicide – a pistol shot, cyanide or even fighting the Soviets to their last breath.

Around 2.30am on April 30, Hitler assembled his staff and bade them a final farewell. At noon, he attended a last military briefing and heard only confirmation of the inevitable. A vegetarian lunch was served two hours later, then the newly married couple spent some quiet moments with Bormann, Propaganda Minister Joseph Goebbels and a few other members of the Nazi inner circle. Shortly after 3pm they retired to their private quarters.

Minutes later, the report of a single shot reverberated through the dank confines of the Führerbunker. After waiting respectfully for a short time, Rochus Misch, a member of Hitler's SS bodyguard, was one of the first to enter the area. He recalled: "Heinz Linge [Hitler's valet] took me to one side and we went in. I saw Hitler slumped by the table. I didn't see any blood

Above: Hitler and Eva Braun pause for a photo at Berchtesgaden during happier times. The Führer's loyal Alsatian, Blondi, is at right. (Creative Commons Bundesarchiv Bild via Wikimedia Commons)

Below: SS officer Erich Kempka, shown driving the Führer and Italian dictator Benito Mussolini, was a player in the final drama of Hitler's suicide. (Creative Commons Bundesarchiv Bild via Wikimedia Commons)

STATE OF WAR

After two weeks of fighting and the turn of the new year, the Nazi lightning bolt of the Ardennes Offensive had been blunted and then reversed. Some mopping up remained through January 1945, but the last gasp of real, threatening German military might in the West was defeated.

Although few would have thought the outcome of World War Two in Europe had hung in the balance, the Battle of the Bulge called into question the assumption of a rather uneventful victory with Allied forces 'running out the clock' as they marched inexorably across the Fatherland. In the wake of the defeat of the Ardennes Offensive, the Allies emerged with a new resolve, a grim determination to 'pay the butcher's bill' in dead and wounded but to finish the job once and for all.

Allied armies moved rapidly towards the great River Rhine, the last natural barrier protecting the German homeland from outright invasion from the West. Field Marshal Bernard Montgomery's 21st Army Group crossed the river at the town of Wesel during Operation Plunder. General Omar Bradley's 12th Army Group made its historic crossing at Remagen, where the Ludendorff railway bridge had been seized, remarkably intact, at Oppenheim south of the German city of Mainz, and elsewhere. General Dwight Eisenhower, Supreme Command of Allied Forces in Western Europe, chose not to advance on Berlin. His reasoning was sound. The city would be left for the Soviet Red Army to conquer while the Western Allied forces concentrated on securing the industrial nexus of the Ruhr and destroying any armed resistance.

On the Eastern Front, the Red Army, a veritable juggernaut, had turned the tide against the invading Nazis in 1944, the fabled year of Joseph Stalin's "ten blows". The vengeful Soviets had suffered like no other nation in opposition to the Nazis, losing millions of military personnel and civilians to the invaders who had occupied much of their land, Belorussia, Russia, Ukraine, the Baltic States and more, for an agonising two years or longer.

Once the momentum had shifted in the East, Germans everywhere quaked at the prospect of Soviet soldiers occupying their territory and exacting vengeance. The German nightmare scenario was becoming increasingly real during the early months of 1945 as the Red Army ejected the Wehrmacht from Soviet territory and chased, fought, battered and bled to the frontiers of the Third Reich, liberating the great capitals of Eastern Europe in the process. The Nazis fought like lions, but were overmatched.

Finally, at the end of April, the Red Army was in the streets of Berlin, tearing at the heart of the Nazi Reich. Soviet soldiers brought the Wagnerian Götterdämmerung home to the German capital. Their fury induced the Nazi Führer Adolf Hitler to put a gun to his head and end his own life. Responsible for the deaths of millions, Hitler, even in his last hours on Earth, refused to own the holocaust he had initiated and blamed his victims and the German people for their failure to achieve the domination of the so-called master race. The depth of Nazi depravity was laid bare to the world in the discovery of numerous death camps, murder factories where millions of innocent people were tortured, shot and dispatched in gas chambers.

The Marine Corps Memorial in Arlington, Virginia, commemorates the raising of the US flag on Iwo Jima's Mount Suribachi. (Felix Weldon Public Domain Government of the United States via Wikimedia Commons)

Destined for defeat, German officers review a map during their advance towards the River Meuse in the Battle of the Bulge. (Creative Commons Bundesarchiv Bild via Wikimedia Commons)

Soviet soldiers and tanks race across an open plain during the battle for Budapest, capital of Hungary. (Government of Ukraine via Wikimedia Commons)

An American soldier crouches on the heights above the Ludendorff railway bridge crossing the River Rhine at Remagen. (US Army Signal Corps via Wikimedia Commons)

With Allied armies marching towards victory, the leaders of the US, Britain and the Soviet Union had met at the Crimean resort of Yalta on the Black Sea to discuss the future of the post-war world. Two months later, President Franklin D Roosevelt was dead at 63. The free world mourned; 'FDR' was eulogised and lauded. And there was unfinished business to conclude.

In the Pacific, the Japanese government and military establishment shared, at least for a time during the early months of 1945, the experience of cultural denial. They reasoned that victory was still achievable, even in the face of overwhelming American and Allied military strength that moved inexorably across the vast ocean expanse towards the home islands of Japan.

As the days wore on and American bombing raids devastated Japanese cities, burning wide swaths of territory to the ground and killing thousands, the amphibious campaign continued. Three divisions of US Marines stormed ashore on Iwo Jima, known also as Sulphur Island for the pervasive acrid odour of the element. For more than a month, they battled tenacious defenders willing to die for their emperor. The Japanese were ensconced in a warren of tunnels interconnecting along underground routes between machine gun nests, artillery emplacements, bunkers and pillboxes. They poked the barrels of guns from the mouths of caves and fired incessantly until silenced by flamethrower, satchel charge, Marine heroism and even bulldozer.

Four days into the agonising fight for Iwo Jima, a Marine patrol fought its way to the top of Mount Suribachi, planted the US flag for the world to see and created one of the iconic images of men at war at any time in any place. Captured by Associated Press photographer Joe Rosenthal, the photo of the flag-raising electrified the world. US Secretary of the Navy James Forrestal witnessed the moment and later declared: "The raising of that flag on Suribachi means a Marine Corps for the next 500 years."

Thirty-seven days after the flag was raised on Suribachi, April 1, 1945, US Marines and Army soldiers stormed ashore on the island of Okinawa in the Ryukyus archipelago, the doorstep of the home islands of Japan. The landings were virtually unopposed, but the storm broke with unprecedented intensity. At the end of the month, the fight for Okinawa still raged. At the same time, the US Navy's Fifth Fleet maintained station off the island, launching air support missions, running supplies, reinforcements and equipment ashore. The sailors also fought for their own lives, braving the onslaught of the Kamikaze as swarms of Japanese suicide pilots tried to crash into the American vessels. The battle off the shores of Okinawa was a veritable typhoon of steel.

The winter and spring of 1945 brought desperation, hope and destruction in waves. But by the end of April, the days of the Third Reich were literally fewer than the fingers counted on two hands. As for Japan, destruction on a grand scale – more terrible than had ever been contemplated – lay in store.

Soldiers of the US Army's 96th Infantry Division fight the determined Japanese defenders on Okinawa. (US Army Signal Corps via Wikimedia Commons)

Smoke and flame billow from the aircraft carrier USS *Intrepid*, struck by a Japanese Kamikaze suicide aircraft off Okinawa. (US Navy National Museum of Naval Aviation via Wikimedia Commons)

MURDER OF THE GOEBBELS CHILDREN

With the assistance of SS dentist Helmut Kunz, Magda Goebbels, wife of Propaganda Minister Joseph Goebbels and an ardent Nazi, sedated her six children, five girls and a boy ranging in age from four to 12, and then murdered them with poison. Accounts are at odds as to whether the children were first given a sweet beverage laced with chemical compound or injected with morphine to induce a deep sleep before they were killed.

Joseph and Magda Goebbels had brought their family into the damp, grey existence of the Führerbunker on April 22 to occupy four rooms, and none would emerge from the dark existence alive. A few days later, Frau Goebbels penned a letter to Luftwaffe Lieutenant Harald Quandt, her son from a previous marriage who had been taken prisoner in North Africa.

"My beloved son!" Magda wrote. "By now we have been in the Führerbunker for six days already – daddy, your six little siblings, and I, for the sake of giving our National Socialistic lives the only possible honourable end... You shall know that I stayed here against daddy's will, and that even last Sunday the Führer wanted to help me to get out. You know your mother – we have the same blood, for me there was no wavering.

"Our glorious idea is ruined and with it everything beautiful and marvellous that I have known in my life. The world that comes after the Führer and National Socialism is no longer worth living in and therefore I took the children with me, for they are too good for the life that would follow, and a merciful God will understand me when I will give them salvation..."

Days before Magda's heinous act, she had denied the children the opportunity to be evacuated from the unfolding scene of horror. Famed Nazi test pilot Hanna Reitsch had pleaded to fly them out of Berlin to safety – to no avail. "My God! Frau Goebbels, the children cannot stay here!" Reitsch had said, but her entreaties had fallen on

German test pilot Hanna Reitsch pleaded for the lives of the Goebbels children in the Führerbunker. (Creative Commons Bundesarchiv Bild via Wikimedia Commons)

deaf ears. Helga, Holdein, Hildegard, Helmut, Hedwig and Heidrun, were sacrificed on the altar of Nazism by their deranged parents.

After their children were dead, Magda and Joseph Goebbels reportedly took cyanide. They were finished off with pistol shots to the head, as they had instructed a trusted aide to perform the grim task. In a last effort at dark humour, Joseph had joked that he would walk up the stairs to the garden of the Reich Chancellery so that others would not have to carry his corpse.

The partially burned bodies of Joseph and Magda Goebbels and their six children were soon discovered by Soviet soldiers and easily identified.

Frau Magda Goebbels, shown here with husband Nazi Propaganda Minister Joseph Goebbels, murdered her six children on May 1, 1945. (Creative Commons Bundesarchiv Bild via Wikimedia Commons)

With the exception of Lieutenant Harald Quandt, the Goebbels family died in the Führerbunker. (Creative Commons Bundesarchiv Bild via Wikimedia Commons)

FALL OF BERLIN

Above: Officers of the Red Army 1st Ukrainian Front participate in a victory parade in Moscow. (Creative Commons Ministry of Defence of the Russian Federation via Wikimedia Commons)

Below: Soviet Red Army Marshals Georgy Zhukov and Ivan Konev discuss operations against the Germans. (Creative Commons Ministry of Defence of the Russian Federation via Wikimedia Commons)

The Soviet Red Army battled in the streets of Berlin for nearly a week, and the rivalry between Marshal Georgy Zhukov, commander of the 1st Belorussian Front, and Ivan Konev commanding the 1st Ukrainian Front, had been so heated that at times their troops may well have fired on one another. By early May, the fight for the city was over. For the defenders, it had been a harrowing ordeal, but the Hammer and Sickle banner was flying from the Reichstag and the Führer was dead. On May 2, 1945, the capital of Nazi Germany was finally in the hands of its sworn enemy.

The last chapter of the battle for Berlin had begun with fury on April 26. The 8th Guards and 1st Guards Tank Armies fought their way through the first and second defensive rings, crossing the S-Bahn public transportation line with the 8th Guards Army taking control of Tempelhof Airport. To the west, elements of the 1st Belorussian Front fought for two days and entered Charlottenburg while reaching the River Spree. Soviet troops and tanks advanced inexorably towards the centre of Berlin on four primary axes, along the Frankfurter Allee from the southeast, Sonnenallee from the south towards the Belle-Alliance-Platz, again from the south towards the Potsdamer Platz and from the north to the Reichstag, where the German Parliament had once convened and that had not been in use since a devastating fire had gutted the building in 1933.

On April 28, Soviet soldiers captured the Potsdamerstrasse Bridge across the Landwehr Canal, and fighting spread into the wide residential area of the Tiergarten, home to the Berlin Zoo. Early the next morning the 3rd Shock Army crossed the Moltke Bridge over the River Spree. The Reichstag was situated to the left fronting the Konigsplatz, which was mined and heavily defended by machine gun nests, artillery, a handful of tanks and an ad hoc force of about 6,000 Germans. The Interior Ministry building was steadily under attack and progress was sluggish. At daybreak on April 30, Red Army troops occupied Gestapo headquarters on Prinz Albrechtstrasse briefly, but a German counterattack forced them to retire. Nevertheless, the Soviets did take control of most of the diplomatic quarter by the end of the day.

The 79th Rifle Corps, meanwhile, began an all-out assault against the Reichstag. While soldiers of the 150th Rifle Division dashed across the Konigsplatz to attack the old building frontally, other units struck at its flanks in three unsuccessful attempts in the afternoon. Trundling into the Konigsplatz, Soviet tanks and self-propelled assault guns blasted German positions. At mid-afternoon, a false report flashed round the word that that a Red banner was flying above the Reichstag, but the attackers had managed to advance only a short distance across the Konigsplatz. Major General Vasily Shatilov, commanding the 150th Rifle Division, ordered the attacks to be stepped up.

By 6pm, Soviet soldiers renewed the assault, carrying small mortars to blast open entryways that had been covered with brick and mortar. Once inside, they clashed with Germans in hand-to-hand combat throughout the building. A small group of Red Army soldiers worked their way around the back and found a stairway to the roof. Sergeants Mikhail Yegorov and Meliton Kantaria rushed forward with a Red banner and found an equestrian statue at the roofline. Minutes before 11pm, they jammed the staff into a space in the statue.

Despite the Red banner flying from its height, the Reichstag building was not declared secure until May 2, the last day of the Battle of Berlin. The historic flag-raising was re-enacted for newsreel cameras and still photographers a day later.

Pockets of German troops stubbornly continued the fight on April 30, but General Helmuth Weidling, commanding the defences, had informed Hitler that morning that the Red Army would be in control of the city centre in hours. Perhaps the news

A Soviet 203mm B-4 self-propelled howitzer fires at a German target in a Berlin neighbourhood. (Creative Commons Марк Редькин via Wikimedia Commons)

hastened the Führer's suicide later in the day. The Soviet 5th Shock, 8th Guards, and 8th Guards Tank Armies advanced down the famed Unter den Linden boulevard, approaching the Reich Chancellery and the Führerbunker. Before committing suicide, Hitler authorised General Weidling to attempt a breakout from the encirclement that had formed. But it was no use.

By the evening, only about 10,000 German soldiers remained in defensive positions as Soviet troops and tanks closed in from every direction. Red Army guns pounded the dwindling number of defenders, shelling the Air Ministry building on the Wilhelmstrasse, a strong structure reinforced with steel, concrete and barricades. The 3rd Shock Army raced along the northern edge of the Tiergarten fighting a clutch of German tanks, contacting the 8th Guards Army, and bisecting Berlin.

On May 1, General Hans Krebs, chief of the German General Staff, contacted General Vasily Chuikov, commander of the Soviet 8th Guards Army, informing Chuikov of Hitler's death and asking for surrender terms. Chuikov insisted on unconditional surrender, but Krebs balked, responding that his authority was limited. By then, unit cohesion among the Germans had begun to evaporate. Some soldiers fled, hoping to find American or British lines to surrender rather than giving up to the ruthless Red Army. A relative few escaped the Soviets, crossing the Charlotten Bridge over the River Havel.

At 1am on May 2, Weidling sent another communiqué to Gen Chuikov asking for a second surrender discussion. He was escorted to Chuikov's headquarters and surrendered within the hour. Weidling ordered all German troops to follow suit and put the directive in writing at Chuikov's request. He also made a recording of the order for Soviet trucks to blare through the shattered streets.

Some pockets of fanatical SS troops fought to the death, but at the fortified Berlin Zoo flak tower, about 350 dazed German soldiers finally laid down their weapons and stumbled into captivity and an uncertain future. Berlin had become an occupied city.

A destroyed Soviet IS-2 heavy tank lies before the fortified flak tower at the Berlin Zoo. (Government of Poland Public Domain via Wikimedia Commons)

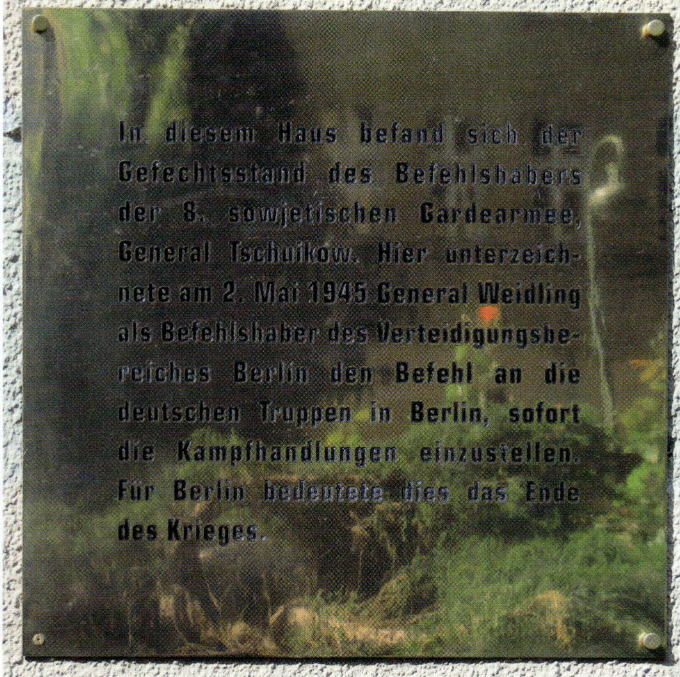

A plaque commemorates the final surrender of German forces defending Berlin to the Soviet Red Army. (Creative Commons OTFW, Berlin via Wikimedia Commons)

Right: General Helmuth Weidling commanded the doomed defence of the city of Berlin. (Creative Commons Bundesarchiv Bild via Wikimedia Commons)

LIBERATION OF RANGOON

A Stuart light tank of an Indian cavalry regiment enters the city of Rangoon, 1945. (Collections of the Imperial War Museums via Wikimedia Commons)

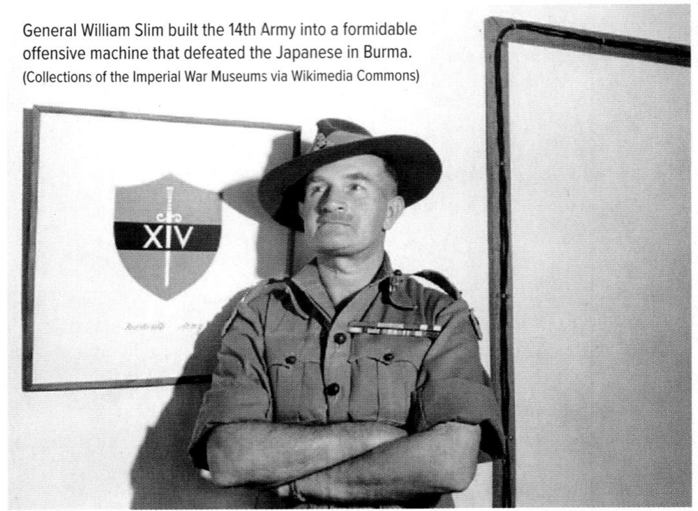

General William Slim built the 14th Army into a formidable offensive machine that defeated the Japanese in Burma. (Collections of the Imperial War Museums via Wikimedia Commons)

Nearly three years after being soundly defeated in Burma and losing Rangoon to the swiftly advancing Japanese, Commonwealth forces returned to the Burmese capital, evacuated by the enemy, as soldiers of the Indian 26th Division marched into the city, brushing aside only token resistance.

After the liberation of Mandalay on March 20, 1945, General William Slim's 14th Army was poised to complete the victory of his Burma campaign. However, he found his forces in the midst of two races simultaneously. One of these was against nature – the vanguard of the 14th Army might bog down with the coming of torrential rains during the annual monsoon season. The other was against competing British forces prosecuting a separate amphibious movement, Operation Dracula, championed by Lord Louis Mountbatten, Supreme Allied Commander of Southeast Asia Command.

Slim sent his forces south along the valleys of the great Rivers Irrawaddy and Sittang. Much of the advance encountered only limited Japanese resistance, and its swiftness meant reliance on resupply by air. Pockets of enemy fighters were sometimes bypassed and mopped up by follow-on 14th Army formations. In mid-April, a highly successful commando thrust was launched to disrupt Japanese communications and supply lines. During Operation Character an estimated 10,000 enemy soldiers were killed while only 60 British Commandos were lost.

The focal point of Japanese resistance was at Pegu, where the Indian IV Corps encountered the enemy

105th Independent Mixed Brigade, under General Hideji Matsui. After destroying key bridges and obliging the IV Corps, commanded by General Frank Messervy, to fight, Matsui withdrew under orders to defend Rangoon. Instead, the Indian 17th Division forced his remaining troops to retreat into the surrounding hills. Meanwhile, General Heitaro Kimura, commanding Japanese forces in Burma, evacuated Rangoon at the end of April. As the monsoon rains started, Slim's 14th Army spearheads were still 50 miles north of the Burmese capital. As they ground steadily toward the Burmese capital from the landward side, Operation Dracula was set in motion.

Major General Henry Chambers' Indian 26th Division executed the initial amphibious landing of Operation Dracula on May 2. The offensive was supported by overwhelming naval forces of the Royal Navy 21st Aircraft Carrier Squadron, sailing from Trincomalee, Ceylon, along with the battleships *Richelieu* and *Queen Elizabeth* and their escorts. Air support included 12 squadrons of American medium bombers and the aircraft of No. 224 Group, Royal Air Force.

A day after landing, the 26th Indian Division entered Rangoon virtually unopposed. On May 6, 1945, these troops and the 17th Indian Division, 14th Army made contact near the village of Hlegu, effectively ending the campaign.

An artillery piece is offloaded near Rangoon during Operation Dracula, May 1945. (Collections of the Imperial War Museums via Wikimedia Commons)

JAPANESE BALLOON BOMB KILLS CIVILIANS

Twenty-six-year-old Elyse Mitchell, five months pregnant, was killed in an explosion along with five children, members of the youth group at the Christian and Missionary Alliance Church of Bly, Oregon. The origin of the explosion was a curious but lethal weapon, a Japanese Fu-Go balloon bomb that had made its way at high altitude, riding the jet stream across the Pacific and descending to the forest floor on Gearhart Mountain in southern Oregon.

Archie Mitchell, Elyse's husband, had recently been appointed church minister, and plans for the day included a short fishing trip to allow the couple to acquaint themselves with some of the young members of the church. After driving some distance down a forest service road through land owned by the Weyerhaeuser Timber Company, Archie was informed by a work crew that the road ahead was impassable. While he talked with the crew, Elyse and the children stretched their legs, walking a bit off the road. She called to Archie that the group had stumbled across something curious, and he shouted back that he would take a look after moving the car.

Moments later, the fatal explosion rocked the surrounding area. Archie and men of the work crew rushed to the scene and found the lifeless bodies of the children surrounding a sizable crater. Elyse died moments later. These unfortunate victims were the only casualties of the Japanese Fu-Go balloon bomb programme undertaken in 1942 in response to the famed Doolittle Raid, conducted in April of that year by US medium bombers flying from the aircraft carrier USS *Hornet* and dropping bombs on Tokyo and environs.

Both the Japanese Army and Navy developed balloon bombs, made of paper or rubber, and intended to use the prevailing winds to reach North America, particularly the Pacific Northwest where it was hoped they would ignite major forest fires. In the event, more than 6,000 balloons were launched either from the home islands of Japan or from submarines at sea, beginning in 1944. Most of them failed to create any disturbance, becoming lost or falling to Earth in remote areas that left them undiscovered. As for forest fires, heavy rains and winter snows significantly reduced the likelihood of a conflagration.

However, by the end of World War Two in the Pacific, more than 300 encounters with the Fu-Go balloons were reported. While most of the balloon bombs did come down in the Pacific Northwest, including 57 in Canadian British Columbia, 37 in Alaska, 45 in Oregon and 28 in Washington, others travelled remarkably long distances and were reported as far east as Texas, Kansas and Michigan.

Workers attempt to remove a Japanese balloon bomb that has descended near Nixon, Nevada, March 29, 1945. (National Museum of the US Navy via Wikimedia Commons)

A Japanese Fu-Go balloon bomb is shown aloft after being reinflated in California for evaluation. (US Army via Wikimedia Commons)

This monument was erected in memory of the civilians who died in the explosion of a Fu-Go balloon bomb on May 5, 1945. (Creative Commons Michael (a.k.a. moik) McCullough via Wikimedia Commons)

NAZI GERMANY SURRENDERS UNCONDITIONALLY

Colonel General Alfred Jodl signs the instrument of surrender at Reims, France, May 7, 1945.
(Franklin D Roosevelt Presidential Library and Museum via Wikimedia Commons)

A German military delegation signed the instrument of surrender ending World War Two in Europe in the predawn hours of May 7, 1945. The surrender was conducted in a schoolhouse in the city of Reims, 80 miles northeast of Paris.

At the direction of Admiral Karl Dönitz, successor to Hitler as leader of Nazi Germany, the Chief of Staff of the German High Command Colonel General Alfred Jodl signed for his defeated military. Jodl was accompanied by his aide, Major Wilhelm Oxenius, and Admiral Hans-Georg von Friedeburg, deputy commander of the Kriegsmarine U-boat force and last chief of the German Navy. General Walter Bedell Smith, Chief of Staff of SHAEF (Supreme Headquarters Allied Expeditionary Force) signed for the Western Allies.

Other American officers in attendance were General Omar Bradley, commander of the 12th Army Group, General Jacob Devers commanding the 6th Army Group, General Carl Spaatz commanding Strategic Air Forces in Europe, and Assistant Chief of Staff General Harold Bull. Representing the British military were deputy commander of SHAEF Air Chief Marshal Sir Arthur Tedder, Admiral Sir Harold Burroughs as Assistant Chief of Staff Royal Navy, SHAEF Deputy Chief of Staff General Fred Morgan, and Air Marshal Sir J M Robb as the Deputy Chief of Staff (Air). French General Francois Sevez represented his government, and General Ivan Susloparov represented the Soviet high command (Stavka).

The documents were signed with a Parker 51 fountain pen owned by General Dwight D Eisenhower, the SHAEF Supreme Commander. Eisenhower's disdain for the Nazis was readily apparent – he refused to meet with the German delegates for any lengthy period, and when Jodl was brought before him after signing the surrender documents, the reception was curt and direct.

Eisenhower later recalled: "I said, 'You will, officially and personally, be held responsible if the terms of this surrender are violated, including its provisions for the German commanders to appear in Berlin at the moment set by the Russian high command to accomplish the formal surrender to that government. That is all.' He saluted and left."

The Reims surrender was not the first to Allied forces in the West. On May 2, German troops in Italy capitulated at Caserta and, on May 4, German troops in the Netherlands, Denmark and northwest Germany surrendered to Field Marshal Bernard Montgomery and the 21st Army Group. The formal Nazi surrender to the Soviet Union was concluded in Berlin on May 9.

Following the Reims surrender, several SHAEF staff officers attempted to compose an appropriate communiqué announcing the end of hostilities. Eisenhower scrapped every message and then wrote one himself: "The mission of this Allied Force was fulfilled at 0241, local time, May 7th, 1945. Signed, Eisenhower."

At Reims, General Dwight D Eisenhower and other Allied officers discuss the surrender of the Germans. The SHAEF supreme commander holds his Parker pen used to sign. (US Army via Wikimedia Commons)

This painting by artist Lucien Jonas depicts the surrender proceedings at Reims, May 7, 1945.
(Museum of Fine Arts Reims via Wikimedia Commons)

VE DAY

Within hours of the German surrender in a schoolhouse in Reims, France, the news that World War Two in Europe was over flashed around the globe. A second surrender ceremony took place in Moscow at the insistence of the Soviet government, but celebrations proclaiming VE Day (Victory in Europe Day), May 8, 1945, were already under way in cities and rural areas around the world.

In London, King George VI and Queen Elizabeth were accompanied by their daughters Elizabeth and Margaret, stepping onto the balcony at Buckingham Palace to acknowledge the cheers of a delirious throng. At 9pm that evening, the King took to the radio to address the nation. His comments reflected the joy of the moment but acknowledged that the war in the Pacific was continuing. Even as he delivered the address, his daughters had dressed discreetly and gone into the city's streets to experience the revelry for themselves.

"Today we give thanks to Almighty God for a great deliverance," the King said. "Speaking from our Empire's oldest capital city, war-battered but never for one moment daunted or dismayed – speaking

President Harry Truman prepares to address the American people on VE Day. (National Archives and Records Administration via Wikimedia Commons)

from London, I ask you to join with me in that act of thanksgiving. Germany, the enemy who drove all Europe into war, has been finally overcome. In the Far East we have yet to deal with the Japanese, a determined and cruel foe. To this we shall turn with the utmost resolve and with all our resources. But at this hour, when the dreadful shadow of war has passed from our hearths and homes in these islands, we may at last make one pause for thanksgiving and then turn our thoughts to the tasks all over the world which peace in Europe brings with it."

Prime Minister Winston Churchill, after appearing at Buckingham Palace with the royal family, headed to Whitehall and addressed another jubilant crowd. "God bless you all," he declared. "This is your victory. In our long history, we have never seen a greater day than this. Everyone, man or woman, has done their best."

In Washington DC, President Harry Truman issued a proclamation that captured the moment: "Much remains to be done. The victory won in the West must now be won in the East. The whole world must be cleansed of the evil from which half the world has been freed. United, the peace-loving nations have demonstrated in the West that their arms are stronger by far than the might of dictators or

Above: Prime Minister Winston Churchill waves to the crowd in Whitehall on VE Day, May 8, 1945. (Collections of the Imperial War Museums via Wikimedia Commons)

Below: Jubilant Londoners celebrate Victory in Europe on May 8, 1945. (Collections of the Imperial War Museums via Wikimedia Commons)

the tyranny of military cliques that once called us soft and weak. The power of our peoples to defend themselves against all enemies will be proved in the Pacific as it has been proved in Europe. For the triumph of spirit and of arms which we have won, and of its promise to peoples everywhere who join us in the love of freedom, it is fitting that we, as a nation, give thanks to Almighty God, who has strengthened us and given us the victory..."

Meanwhile, a huge crowd gathered in New York City's Times Square to celebrate the victory over the Nazis. On Long Island, children paraded through neighbourhoods clanging pots and pans. Newspaper headlines blared the news, and in time there was a collective pause to reflect on the cost of the triumph in lives and treasure.

The celebration brought a tumult of emotion and relief. However, leaders warned that the victory was as yet incomplete. Imperial Japan was everywhere on the defensive but remained defiant, full of fight with many willing to die for their emperor.

SOVIET UNION PROCLAIMS VICTORY DAY

The Soviet Union officially announced the end of World War Two in Europe following a surrender ceremony in the shattered city of Berlin in the first moments of this day.

On May 7, the armed forces of Nazi Germany surrendered to the Allies in a Reims, France, schoolhouse. However, Field Marshal Wilhelm Keitel and a second delegation of high-ranking Nazi military officers were subsequently summoned to the mess hall of the former engineering school at Karlshorst in Berlin, to execute more documents.

The purpose of this ceremony was to conclude the surrender of the German Wehrmacht formally to the Soviet Union. Shortly after the May 7 capitulation at Reims, Soviet Red Army Chief of Staff General Alexei Antonov was concerned that the proceedings had the character of a separate peace with the Western Allies. Fighting continued on the Eastern Front, and the Soviets were aware that many German units opposing them were desperately fleeing westwards hoping to avoid turning their collective fate over to the vengeful Red Army.

Despite the fact that General Dwight D Eisenhower, Supreme Commander of Allied Forces in Western Europe, had rebuffed German overtures for a peace settlement that did not include the Soviet Union, the Kremlin was immovable in its demand. Within six hours of the Reims event, the Soviet government had formally objected to the finality of that surrender. In turn, General Eisenhower agreed to a second ceremony that carried with it the implication that the Soviet Union had borne the heaviest weight of the fighting against the Nazis along with Premier Joseph Stalin's requirement that the highest-ranking German military officers available should sign a surrender document in Berlin.

Keitel was joined by Admiral Hans-Georg von Friedeburg, chief of the Kriegsmarine, and Colonel General Hans-Jürgen Stumpff, commander of the Luftwaffe. Witnesses recalled that Keitel raised his field marshal's baton in salute to Soviet Marshal Georgy Zhukov along with other Allied officers, including the deputy commander of SHAEF (Supreme Headquarters Allied Expeditionary Force) Air Chief Marshal Sir Arthur Tedder, General Carl Spaatz as commander of Strategic Air Forces in Europe, and General Jean de Lattre de Tassigny, commander of the French First Army. They also recalled that the Allied officers did not respond.

The room was filled with representatives of the press and radio, and these surged close to the table as Zhukov motioned for the Germans to come forward and sign the surrender documents. Keitel responded that the documents should be brought to him, and Zhukov snapped to an interpreter: "Tell them to come here to sign."

Keitel removed his gloves with a flourish, and at 11.01pm, local time, the Soviets obtained their satisfactory surrender. The moment was choreographed so that the clock had turned to May 9, 1945, in Moscow, and the Soviets could claim their own day of victory over the Nazis in their Great Patriotic War.

Air Chief Marshal Sir Arthur Tedder reviews an honour guard on arrival in Berlin to attend the German surrender to the Soviets. (National Museum of the US Navy via Wikimedia Commons)

Field Marshal Wilhelm Keitel signs surrender documents in Berlin under the watchful eyes of the Soviets. (National Archives and Records Administration via Wikimedia Commons)

Marshal Georgy Zhukov signs the German surrender documents on behalf of the Soviet Union at Karlshorst in Berlin. (официальная фотосъемка Public Domain via Wikimedia Commons)

REICHSMARSCHALL HERMANN GÖRING CAPTURED

While in custody at Augsburg, Germany, Hermann Göring gives an interview to members of the Allied press corps. (US Air Force via Wikimedia Commons)

nearby castle and others that Göring was taken directly to the headquarters of the 36th Division at the Grand Hotel in Kitzbühel.

Dahlquist, who spoke German, was the first to interrogate Göring, who spoke freely about recent events but offered no information of real value. He discussed the disagreement with Hitler. However, the pressing question regarding the whereabouts of other top Nazis yielded no actionable intelligence.

Göring was eventually placed on trial by the Allied tribunal at Nuremberg. Although he testified in his own defence and proved to be a formidable courtroom adversary, he was found guilty of multiple war crimes and sentenced to death by hanging. But Göring avoided the noose by crushing a cyanide capsule between his teeth on the eve of his execution date, October 15, 1946. The circumstances of the suicide remain the subject of conjecture. The cyanide was believed to have been hidden in a jar of cream in his luggage.

Right: Former high-ranking Nazi and Luftwaffe chief Hermann Göring posed for this photo in June 1945. (US Army Signal Corps via Wikimedia Commons)

Below: A pensive Hermann Göring sits in the prisoners' dock at the International Military Tribunal, Nuremberg. (Harry S Truman Presidential Library and Museum via Wikimedia Commons)

Once wielding immense power in Germany, second only to that of Führer Adolf Hitler in the Nazi hierarchy, Reichsmarschall Hermann Göring surrendered to elements of the US Seventh Army at Radstadt, Austria, southeast of Salzburg.

Chief of the Luftwaffe, Göring had also held numerous offices within the Third Reich, including recognition as Hitler's probable successor as leader of Nazi Germany. He was also responsible for issuing orders that set the horror of the Holocaust in motion, resulting in the deaths of millions of Jews and other ethnic Europeans.

On April 23, 1945, Göring had fallen out of favour with Hitler and been stripped of all offices, ranks and medals. He had dared to assert authority separate from that of the Führer and intended to take full power in the Reich. Nevertheless, Göring maintained prominence among the Nazi leaders who were sought in the last days of World War Two and its immediate aftermath.

On this day, Göring dispatched his aide, Colonel Bernd von Brauchitsch, to negotiate with American officers of the 36th Infantry Division, for terms of the famous figure's surrender. Brauchitsch reached the 36th Division command post with a message for General Dwight D Eisenhower, Supreme Allied Commander in Western Europe, as well as General Jacob Devers commanding the US Sixth Army Group. He explained the situation to 36th Division commander General John Dahlquist and assistant commander General Robert I Stack.

Brauchitsch extended an offer to send his driver and General Stack back to Göring's hiding place, and en route the high-ranking Nazi was found along the road with his wife, Emmy, and daughter, Edda. Accounts vary as to where the group went next, some asserting that the night was spent at a

BATTLE OF THE MALACCA STRAIT

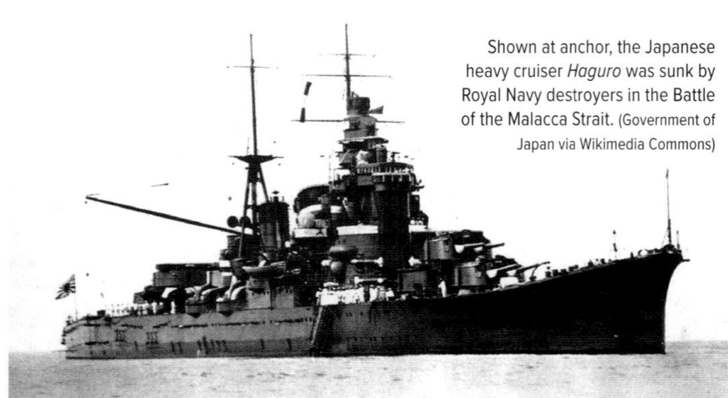

Shown at anchor, the Japanese heavy cruiser *Haguro* was sunk by Royal Navy destroyers in the Battle of the Malacca Strait. (Government of Japan via Wikimedia Commons)

In one of last significant naval surface actions of World War Two in the Pacific, elements of the British Royal Navy sank the Japanese heavy cruiser *Haguro* and damaged its escorting destroyer, *Kamikaze*, in exchange for damage to the destroyer HMS *Saumarez* and the loss of two ratings killed and three seriously wounded.

In early May 1945, the British East Indies Fleet, based at Trincomalee, Ceylon, undertook two complementary missions, Operation Mitre and Operation Dukedom, across the Malacca Strait and the South Andaman Sea. The former was intended to hunt down and sink Japanese auxiliary and transport vessels, while the latter was specifically aimed at *Haguro*. The Japanese cruiser had been utilised as a supply ship to replenish the increasingly isolated Japanese island garrisons in the Bay of Bengal and the Dutch East Indies.

Intelligence reports received in May indicated that *Haguro* was ordered to sortie through the Malacca Strait, its primary mission the evacuation of the Japanese troops from the Andaman and Nicobar Islands and return them to the major base at Singapore. Three separate British squadrons, designated Force 61, sortied in search of *Haguro*, and submarine reports from HMS *Subtle* and HMS *Statesman* confirmed that the enemy cruiser

was at sea. Japanese air reconnaissance provided an early warning, and *Haguro* retired to Singapore on May 10 without engaging.

Four days later, *Haguro* and *Kamikaze* set out again from Singapore. This time they were located by Royal Navy reconnaissance aircraft and attacks by Grumman Avenger torpedo bombers inflicted slight damage on the Japanese cruiser. Meanwhile, Captain Manley Power, commanding the 26th Destroyer Flotilla, steamed towards the Japanese aboard *Saumarez* in company with V-class destroyers *Virago*, *Vigilant*, *Verulan* and *Venus*.

In a heavy thunderstorm, *Venus* made radar contact with the Japanese at a distance of 39 miles. As Power deployed his destroyers in a crescent formation to spring a trap, *Venus* came into firing position just after 1am, May 15. However, technical difficulties rendered the attack a failure. *Kamikaze* came into view off the starboard bow of *Saumarez*, which opened fire inflicting damage on the Japanese destroyer. But the 8in and 4.7in guns of *Haguro* found the range. A 4.7in shell struck No. 1 boiler room aboard *Saumarez*, failed to explode, but resulted in the British casualties.

In response, three torpedoes from *Saumarez* and *Verulam* slammed into *Haguro*. Three more torpedoes from *Venus* and *Virago* slowed and then stopped *Harugo* dead in the water. Three more, two from *Venus* and another from *Vigilant*, finally sent the battered cruiser to the bottom amid a fusillade of shellfire just after 2am. The damaged *Kamikaze* managed to limp back to Singapore; more than 900 Japanese sailors were killed in the engagement. The only damage suffered by the 26th Destroyer Flotilla was aboard *Saumarez*.

Right: The Royal Navy S-class destroyer HMS *Saumarez* was damaged during the Battle of the Malacca Strait. (Royal Navy Collections of the Imperial War Museums via Wikimedia Commons)

Below: The Royal Navy V-class destroyer HMS *Venus* played a key role in the Battle of the Malacca Strait, May 15, 1945. (Collections of the Imperial War Museums via Wikimedia Commons)

REICHSFÜHRER SS HEINRICH HIMMLER CAPTURED

Perhaps the most wanted of high-ranking Nazi officials still at large, Reichsführer SS Heinrich Himmler – one of the chief planners of the Holocaust and ruthless leader of Hitler's fanatically loyal paramilitary organisation – was captured at a British checkpoint while attempting to flee to safety.

The hunt for Nazi war criminals was vigorous during the days after World War Two in Europe, and while others had surrendered or been rounded up previously, Himmler donned a dirty Wehrmacht sergeant's uniform and an eye patch. He attempted to blend in with thousands of German soldiers trying to return to what was left of their homes. In company with two other German soldiers – both well dressed and continually looking back at the disguised Himmler who lagged behind them – the scene was curious when the trio approached a British checkpoint in Bremervörde, northern Germany.

Himmler's lifeless body lies on the floor of a British Army medical facility after his suicide in May 1945. (Collections of the Imperial War Museums via Wikimedia Commons)

Immediately under suspicion, these Germans were asked to produce identification papers, standard documents that had been distributed by Allied authorities to German soldiers in the days after hostilities ceased. Alerts had been posted that some counterfeit documents intended to assist the escapes of SS personnel were in circulation, further raising the wariness of the checkpoint guards. When the third German, allegedly Sergeant Heinrich Hizinger,

With Deputy Führer Rudolf Hess at his left, Reichsführer Heinrich Himmler views a scale model of the Dachau concentration camp in 1936. (Creative Commons Bundesarchiv Bild via Wikimedia Commons)

presented his documents, they bore the same bogus stamp that has been detected on other falsified papers.

The three Germans were transferred to a detention camp for interrogation and, under questioning, Himmler removed the eye patch and admitted his true identity with the forlorn hope of bargaining for his life. A short time later, Himmler was removed for a medical examination and when the attending physician, Captain C J 'Jimmy' Wells, attempted to look into Himmler's mouth, he noticed a small blue object.

Wells attempted to remove the object, but Himmler bit down on the cyanide capsule he had hidden on his person for many days. Within minutes, the Nazi lies dead on the floor. Himmler had cheated the hangman, depriving the Allies of the proceedings of justice that would have disclosed his personal guilt and depravity to the world. In the end, his complicity in Nazi atrocities was brought to light amid Allied war crimes trials.

Ironically, Himmler had been undone by the document intended to assist in his bid for freedom. The false identity paper survives to this day and is on display at the Military Intelligence Museum, Shefford, Bedfordshire.

Reichsführer SS Heinrich Himmler walks with SS henchmen during a tour of the Mauthausen concentration camp in 1941. (Creative Commons Bundesarchiv Bild via Wikimedia Commons)

SHURI LINE BREACHED ON OKINAWA

7th Marines reached the crest of Dakeshi Ridge and surveyed the tough, rock-strewn Wana Draw and Wana Ridge. An agonising 19 days were required to secure the area, and the Marines lost an average of 200 men for every 100yds gained.

To the west, the 6th Marine Division advanced to a 230ft barren hill that was soon nicknamed Sugar Loaf. Flanked by two smaller hills, dubbed Half Moon and Horseshoe, the terrain's features constituted the nexus of the western Japanese command in the Shuri Line. Two thousand enemy troops confronted the Marines, their fortified positions pre-sighted with interlocking fields of fire. For ten agonising days, the battle for these hills raged, and the summit of Sugar Loaf changed hands several times. After suffering 2,700 casualties, the 6th Marine Division finally controlled most of the complex on May 20.

After days of heavy fighting, General Mitsuru Ushijima, commanding the Japanese forces defending the island of Okinawa in the Ryukyus group, realised that the formidable Shuri Line was at last untenable and withdrew to the final of three defensive perimeters in the southern part of the island.

In early May, General Simon Bolivar Buckner Jr, commanding the US X Corps, had repositioned his troops confronting the heights, deep draws and natural contours of the Shuri Line until they stood poised to attack, four divisions abreast across a 9,000-yard front. In preliminary fighting in the north prior to the realignment, the 1st Marine Division had already taken 1,400 casualties on only six days.

On May 11, Buckner ordered a general attack along the length of the Shuri Line and exhorted his command to pick up the pace of the offensive to relieve pressure on the beleaguered Fifth Fleet, which continued to endure waves of Kamikaze suicide attacks offshore. The 1st Marine Division advanced on the Awacha Pocket, and a week of combat was required to clear that area. The 1st Battalion,

West of the Marine positions, the Army's 96th Division captured Conical Hill, while the 7th Division took Yonabaru.

Ushijima concluded that his flanks were quite vulnerable and issued orders to withdraw from the Shuri Line to his third defensive system, which stretched along numerous fortified hills that dominated the approaches in the extreme southern end of Okinawa to the shores of the East China Sea across the Kiyamu Peninsula. The Japanese took advantage of heavy rains and dense fog to conceal the movement, which was completed with little interference from the Americans.

In the foul weather, tanks of the 6th Marine Division probed their way cautiously into the village of Naha on May 28, and within hours Company A, 1st Battalion, 5th Marines reached the crest of Shuri Ridge without encountering organised opposition. The Marines spilled into the operational sector of the Army's 77th Division and took Ushijima's former headquarters at Shuri Castle on the morning of May 29.

Top: Taken from the position of a Japanese anti-tank gun, the battleground around Sugar Loaf is littered with the debris of close combat. (Government of Japan via Wikimedia Common)

Left: American Marines, one of them poised to fire a bazooka, battle the Japanese outside the village of Naha. (US Marine Corps via Wikimedia Commons)

Right: A US Marine charges a Japanese machine gun position while under heavy fire on Okinawa. (US Marine Corps Archives via Wikimedia Commons)

TYPHOON BATTERS HALSEY'S THIRD FLEET

For the second time in the Pacific War, a typhoon assailed the warships and support vessels of Admiral William F 'Bull' Halsey's Third Fleet. The previous December, high winds and heavy seas sank three destroyers, damaged 27 other ships, destroyed 146 aircraft and resulted in the deaths of 790 US Navy sailors.

This time, the sustained winds of a typhoon later identified as 'Connie' reached 70mph with gusts up to 115mph. The storm buffeted the Third Fleet – Admiral Halsey had received weather alerts of a tropical disturbance approximately 48 hours prior to the onset of the rough conditions. As the hours passed, contradictory reports indicated varying degrees and direction of the approaching storm as elements of Third Fleet engaged in refuelling procedures east of the Philippine Islands. The weather reports covered a 34,000-mile expanse of the Pacific Ocean.

Amid the confusion, Admiral Halsey essentially ordered the ships of the Third Fleet, particularly Task Groups 38.4, 38.1 and 30.8, to continue refuelling and steer into the small but intense typhoon, which had been under meteorological surveillance for at least five days. Halsey believed the typhoon would pass to the east of his command. As the storm intensified, the admiral suspended refuelling. Although the lack of timely reports on the progress of the typhoon and communications delays were contributing factors, it was determined that Halsey was responsible for poor decision-making that led to substantial damage to numerous ships of the Third Fleet and the loss of six lives. Four sailors were seriously injured.

The storm damaged 33 ships while destroying 76 aircraft and damaging 70 others. Task Group 38.4 escaped serious damage, but Task Groups 38.1 and 30.8 were assailed by the extreme conditions, and every ship involved sustained some degree of damage. The heavy cruiser USS *Pittsburgh* was among the most seriously damaged, losing its bow to the raging winds and waters, while two other cruisers received structural damage. In addition, every aircraft carrier was stricken, and USS *Belleau Wood* lost an elevator. The superstructure of the destroyer USS *Samuel*

Workers repair the flight deck of the aircraft carrier USS *Bennington*, damaged during the June 1945 typhoon in the Pacific. (US Navy via Wikimedia Commons)

N Moore was damaged, and the escort aircraft carriers USS *Salamaua* and USS *Windham Bay* each lost portions of their flight decks. The tanker USS *Millicoma* was raked by high winds and structurally damaged.

After this second typhoon incident, the US Navy established more weather stations in the Central Pacific and created the Joint Typhoon Warning Center.

Formal inquiries into the circumstances of the typhoon responses of December 1944 and June 1945 held Admiral Halsey primarily responsible for the damage and loss of life due to errors in judgment committed under the stress of wartime operations, although no negligence was found. Halsey received no substantial censure or punishment.

Its bow section missing after the typhoon of June 5, 1945, the heavy cruiser USS *Pittsburgh* is shown at sea steaming for port and repairs. (US Navy via Wikimedia Commons)

Admiral William F 'Bull' Halsey was found largely responsible for the damage inflicted on the Third Fleet by the typhoon of June 1945. (US Navy via Wikimedia Commons)

AUSTRALIAN FORCES LIBERATE BRUNEI

Above: Smoke rises from Japanese facilities hit by Allied bombers in Brunei prior to the arrival of Australian forces. (US Government via Wikimedia Commons)

Below: Australian 24th Brigade soldiers wade ashore at Labuan on June 10, 1945. (Government of Australia via Wikimedia Commons)

Kesselton, destroying buildings and leaving large fires burning…"

During the general Allied advance in the theatre, Australians had turned their attention to the liberation of the Netherlands East Indies, undertaking a series of operations collectively known as Oboe. The initial Australian landings took place at Tarakan on May 1, 1945, following heavy naval and air bombardment that essentially neutralised most Japanese resistance. The swift capture of the island facilitated Allied air supremacy throughout the region.

After five convoys sortied from ports in the Philippines and Halmahera island group with the main squadron leaving Morotai on June 4, Operation Oboe Six began on June 10 with the landings in northern Borneo at Brunei and Labuan. The troops came ashore at Muara Beach after extensive naval bombardment and mine-clearing efforts were completed. Little opposition was encountered en route to the capital city. The 2/17 Australian Battalion, commanded by Lieutenant Colonel John Broadbent, moved from the northern edge of the beachhead toward the city of Bandar Seri Begawan and made rapid progress towards further objectives as it passed through areas that had been virtually cleared of Japanese forces by the heavy aerial bombing and strafing and the big guns of warships offshore.

Following the significant gains achieved in Oboe One and Oboe Six, Operation Oboe Two was initiated on July 1, 1945. Oboe Two, the last major amphibious assault undertaking by Allied forces during World War Two in the Pacific, involved the landing of 33,000 troops along with accompanying tanks, ground transport, supplies and equipment. The objective of Oboe Two was the city of Balikpapan in eastern Borneo, and the defending Japanese could muster only 2,000 soldiers supplemented by another 3,000 conscripts to oppose the Australian assault. On the first day of Oboe Two, 10,500 Australian troops, 1,950 tons of supplies and 700 vehicles were put ashore. They advanced smartly and liberated the city within hours.

Troops of the 20th and 24th Brigades of the Australian 9th Infantry Division secured the city of Brunei and adjacent Brunei Bay in the north of the island of Borneo, Netherlands East Indies. The victory was significant in the further advance of Allied troops against the occupying Japanese across the Pacific.

General Douglas MacArthur – commander of Allied Forces in the Southwest Pacific – announced the victory in his June 13, 1945, communiqué: "On Borneo, the Australian troops approaching from the north occupied Brunei City, the capital of British Borneo, while on Labuan Island other elements advanced across the island to within a mile of the Timbalai airstrip. Medium and fighter bombers in support swept enemy bivouac and supply areas along the coast to

Australian soldiers of the 2/43 Infantry Battalion cross a river in northern Borneo while on patrol. (Government of Australia via Wikimedia Commons)

OKINAWA DECLARED SECURE

After 82 days of savage fighting, the island of Okinawa in the Ryukyu archipelago, only 340 miles from the Japanese home island of Kyushu, was declared secure.

US Marine General Roy S Geiger made the announcement, having assumed command of the US X Corps following the death of Army General Simon Bolivar Buckner, killed in action by a Japanese shell just four days earlier on June 18. The fight for Okinawa was the bloodiest of World War Two in the Pacific, and Geiger was the only Marine general to command a numbered US army in the conflict. Five days after taking temporary command, Geiger was relieved by Army General Joseph Stilwell.

The battle for Okinawa had entered its final stage after General Mitsuru Ushijima ordered the evacuation of Japanese defensive positions along the heights of the Shuri Line in the south of the island. The defenders retired to their third and final line of fortifications, stretching across Kunishi Ridge to Hill 85, site of Ushijima's headquarters, and then to Hill 95.

During the final push, the 6th Marine Division secured the Oroku Peninsula, annihilating 5,000 enemy troops and securing Naha airfield. The 32nd Regiment of the Army's 7th Infantry Division took Hill 95 on June 12, and the 17th Regiment seized the eastern end of the Yuza Dake escarpment, uncovering the Japanese right flank. The 96th Division moved up to complete the capture of Yuza Dake the following day.

On the western end of the Japanese line, the battle-hardened 1st Marine Division hit Kunishi Ridge, where the 7th Marines were thrown back in early attempts to take the high ground on June 11. Colonel Edward Snedeker organised a surprise night attack that battered its way to the crest of the ridge by sunrise, and the remaining Japanese were shot down while they cooked breakfast. Three Japanese counterattacks failed to dislodge the Marines from Kunishi Ridge and, after five days of fighting, the last organised resistance at the third defensive line was crushed.

The capture of Hill 89 by the 7th Division and Hill 85 by the 77th Division prompted General Geiger to announce that Okinawa was secure on June 22, 1945. Meanwhile, General Ushijima committed ritual suicide along with other Japanese officers and soldiers.

After capturing the Oroku Peninsula, the 6th Marine Division turned southwards to occupy Ara Saki, the southernmost point on Okinawa. Company G, 2nd Battalion, 22nd Marines raised the US flag in the area to signify the hard-won victory.

During the vicious combat, more than 12,000 Americans were killed, while well over 31,000 were wounded and at least 230 were missing. These figures included the casualties of the US Navy, which suffered heavily off Okinawa under repeated Kamikaze attacks. Only 11,000 Japanese from an estimated island garrison of 130,000 were taken prisoner, and deaths among Okinawan civilians were believed to approach 150,000.

A prisoner reads a propaganda leaflet distributed by American troops to calm the fears of Okinawan civilians. (US Army via Wikimedia Commons)

Left: US Marine General Roy S Geiger issued the communiqué stating that Okinawa was secure after 82 days of combat. (US Government via Wikimedia Commons)

Below: Japanese prisoners captured on Okinawa stand under the watchful eye of a guard after the island is secured. (US Marine Corps via Wikimedia Commons)

UNITED NATIONS CHARTER SIGNED

Representatives of 50 countries signed the charter of the United Nations in San Francisco and the document went into effect four months later in October 1945. The charter established the structure of the global body and its guiding principles with the founding members of the security council assuming leading roles. These included the United States, Great Britain, Soviet Union, France and the Republic of China.

Although the League of Nations had been in existence for decades, it was ineffective in preventing the actions of rogue nations bent on conquest in the inter-war years and at the outbreak of World War Two. Prior to US involvement in the war, President Franklin D Roosevelt and Prime Minister Winston Churchill discussed the formation of the United Nations, and the foundational concept was validated in the Atlantic Charter of 1941, as the leaders agreed to work together in promoting a system that would foster world peace and co-operation.

By 1944, the US, Great Britain and the Soviet Union had spearheaded the formation of an alliance of 26 nations to defeat the forces of Nazi Germany, Fascist Italy and Imperial Japan in World War Two. American and British representatives met separately with delegations from the Soviet Union and China in the autumn of that year at Dumbarton Oaks, near Washington DC, to further discuss the purpose and parameters of the proposed United Nations. In February 1945, the idea was raised again during meetings at the Yalta Conference in the Crimea. Two months later, on April 25, during the United Nations Conference on International Organisation, work was undertaken to advance the charter. The text was approved and opened for signatures on June 26, 1945.

The rationale for the United Nations was declared in maintaining world peace and security, developing friendly relations among nations, achieving international co-operation in solving international problems and respect for human rights.

The preamble to the charter reads in part: "WE THE

Above: Delegates to discussions at Dumbarton Oaks near Washington DC pause for a photograph in August 1944. (Schutz Group Photographers (Washington, D.C.), photographer via Wikimedia Commons)

Right: This poster incorporates a few words of the preamble to the United Nations charter. (National Archives and Records Administration via Wikimedia Commons)

Below: US President Harry S Truman addresses the United Nations Conference in San Francisco. (US Government via Wikimedia Commons)

PEOPLE OF THE UNITED NATIONS DETERMINED to save succeeding generations from the scourge of war, which twice in our lifetime has brought untold sorrow to mankind, and to reaffirm faith in the fundamental human rights, in the dignity and worth of the human person, in the equal rights of men and women and of nations large and small, and to establish conditions under which justice and respect for the obligations arising from treaties and other sources of international law can be maintained, and to promote social progress and better standards of life in larger freedom, AND FOR THESE ENDS to practice tolerance and live together in peace with one another as good neighbours, and to unite our strength to maintain international peace and security, and to ensure, by the acceptance of principles and the institution of methods, that armed force shall not be used, save in the common interest, and to employ international machinery for the promotion of the economic and social advancement of all peoples, HAVE RESOLVED TO ACCOMPLISH THESE AIMS..."

CHURCHILL DEFEATED IN GENERAL ELECTION

In the first general elections held since 1935, Clement Attlee and the Labour Party decisively defeated Winston Churchill and the Conservatives. In addition to capturing the prime minister's office, Labour took 393 seats in Parliament while the Conservatives secured only 197. At first, the landslide result seemed thoroughly remarkable since Churchill had led Great Britain through its darkest hour and to victory in World War Two.

However, several factors contributed to the stunning defeat of the Conservatives. The party had focused almost entirely on Churchill as a national hero during the 1945 campaign, while there was an undercurrent of lingering resentment over the Conservative policy of appeasement that contributed directly to the outbreak of war in 1939. Labour, conversely, presented a programme highly influenced by the November 1942 Beveridge Report, published in the autumn of 1942 by the government and principally authored by social economist William Beveridge.

Looking towards the future, the Beveridge Report provided a road map for the evolution of the post-war welfare state in the United Kingdom. Labour offered a war-weary people the prospect of improved workers' rights, social reforms, a commitment to full employment and national healthcare.

Churchill personally contributed to the sweeping change with campaign rhetoric that characterised Labour policies as

Above left: In the July 5, 1945 general election, Clement Attlee and Labour ousted Churchill and the Conservatives from power. (Government of the United Kingdom via Wikimedia Commons)

Above right: After the Labour victory in the 1945 general election, Prime Minister Clement Attlee meets with King George VI. (Collections of the Imperial War Museums via Wikimedia Commons)

reminiscent of the villainous Nazi Gestapo, and the people may well have grown tired of the wartime coalition government that had been in place for a decade. Both were symptomatic of the natural political forces that emerged during the months immediately following the end of World War Two in Europe. Besides, the British armed forces were still engaged in the war in the Pacific against the Japanese.

Historians have analysed the uncertain mood of the British people in mid-1945 and concluded that Churchill's government was closely associated with the austerity and privations of the war years, including food rationing and restrictions on travel. They may simply have wanted to entertain prospects for a better life. Social reforms had been on the discussion table before the war and then set aside. Voters further remembered the political Churchill of the 1910s and 1920s and were unsure exactly what the veteran politician would stand for in the post-war era. He was a member of the elite ruling class, and the people were sceptical that such values were in their best interests.

Following his ousting from office, Churchill remained active as the leader of the opposition. He acknowledged the threat of post-war Soviet expansion and warned of the Cold War struggle that loomed. In 1946, he travelled to the United States for three months and, during a memorable address at Westminster College in Fulton, Missouri, he remarked: "From Stettin in the Baltic to Trieste in the Adriatic, an Iron Curtain has descended across the continent."

Ever resilient, Churchill stood for election again in 1951. The Conservatives regained power and once more the icon of 20th century British politics became prime minister.

Winston Churchill makes his final address during the 1945 campaign at Walthamstow Stadium, East London. (Collections of the Imperial War Museums via Wikimedia Commons)

TRINITY ATOMIC BOMB TEST AT ALAMOGORDO

The world's first atomic bomb detonation lights up the sky at the Trinity site in the New Mexico desert, July 16, 1945. (United States Department of Energy via Wikimedia Commons)

Scientist Dr J Robert Oppenheimer (bending, centre) and General Leslie Groves (centre right) examine the remains of the tower at the Trinity site sometime after the atomic bomb test. (US Army Signal Corps via Wikimedia Commons)

Under the military command of General Leslie Groves and the scientific leadership of University of California theoretical physicist Dr J Robert Oppenheimer, the Manhattan Project had been under way for about two years. A collection of the world's most capable scientists had collaborated on the development of an atomic bomb, nicknamed "the gadget".

While support facilities have been constructed at Oak Ridge, Tennessee, and Hanford, Washington, the scientists conducted their research and experimentation at a remote, purpose-built site at Los Alamos, New Mexico. On this date, they were driven more than 200 miles south of Los Alamos to Alamogordo in the Jomada del Muerto Desert of New Mexico, about 35 miles from the town of Socorro. (Jomada del Muerto translates from the Spanish as 'Journey of the Dead Man'.)

The purpose of the excursion was to observe the test detonation of the world's first atomic bomb codenamed Trinity. The scientists, military officers and other dignitaries crowded into bunkers reinforced with concrete and steel and distanced about 10,000yds (more than five miles) from ground zero. They were provided with dark glasses to shield their eyes from the expected intense flash of light and surge of heat that accompanied the detonation. The Y-1561 bomb, a fission, implosion-type weapon using plutonium 239 and nicknamed 'Fat Man' due to its size, was suspended from the top of a 100ft steel tower.

Countdown began at 5.10am, and the massive explosion was triggered 19 minutes later. A brilliant glow illuminated the sky in a radius of 20 miles as an enormous fireball erupted with smoke and flame billowing skyward to an estimated altitude of 10,000ft. Windows were shattered in the town of Gallup, New Mexico, 225 miles distant, and the light from the detonation was visible 100 miles away. From

the desert floor, the resulting radioactive cloud towered to more than 41,000ft. The atomic payload was equivalent to about 20,000 tons of TNT.

Oppenheimer was awestruck by the sight. He whispered a verse from the *Bhaghavad Gita*, the holy book of the Hindu faith: "Now I am become Death, the destroyer of worlds."

While attending the Potsdam Conference, President Harry Truman received news of the successful Trinity test on July 17, 1945, from Secretary of War Henry L Stimson. On July 31, while the conference was still under way, the president gave Stimson a handwritten note authorising the use of the atomic bomb against Japan no sooner than August 2. Truman also disclosed the existence of the nuclear weapon to Soviet Premier Josef Stalin.

This simple obelisk marks the Trinity site, where the world's first atomic bomb was detonated. (US National Park Service via Wikimedia Commons)

POTSDAM CONFERENCE BEGINS

L to R, British Prime Minister Winston Churchill, President Harry S Truman, and Soviet leader Josef Stalin in the garden of Cecilienhof Palace before meeting for the Potsdam Conference. (National Archives and Records Administration via Wikimedia Commons)

British Prime Minister Clement Attlee, US President Harry Truman, and Soviet Premier Josef Stalin pose for a photograph at Potsdam along with key advisors. (National Museum of the US Navy via Wikimedia Commons)

In the aftermath of World War Two in Europe, the leaders of the United States, the Soviet Union and Great Britain met for their third and final conference at Potsdam, a suburb of the former Nazi capital of Berlin.

Two of the powerful representatives were newcomers. President Harry Truman had been sworn in only in April after the sudden death of Franklin D Roosevelt. Clement Attlee, representing Britain's Labour Party and elected prime minister only 12 days earlier, replaced Winston Churchill while the meetings were under way. By the end of the Potsdam Conference on August 2, 1945, only Soviet Premier Josef Stalin remained of the original 'Big Three'.

The discussions at Potsdam centred on the administration of the recently defeated Germany, the future governments of eastern European nations, and the final defeat of Japan. The leaders were confronted with numerous challenges. Among these were the de-Nazification of Germany, including the removal of signs and symbols of the vanquished Third Reich, the eradication of Nazi ideology among the people, the apprehension and prosecution of Nazi war criminals and senior leaders, and the care and repatriation of thousands of refugees and former prisoners of war across Europe.

The future government of Poland was a particularly contentious issue at Potsdam, as Stalin favoured the pro-Communist government installed in Warsaw with the occupation of the country by the Red Army while the US and Britain endorsed the former Polish government-in-exile then in London. Stalin promised to allow free elections in Poland as well as other eastern European countries then under Soviet military occupation and administrative rule. However, he failed to follow through and Communist regimes were installed in Bulgaria, Hungary, Romania, and Czechoslovakia, as well as Poland. Other issues relating to eastern Europe involved the resettlement of thousands of ethnic Germans, expelled from territories that many had occupied under the Nazi program of Lebensraum, or living space, in the East.

The question of war reparations from Germany was discussed, and Stalin reaffirmed a commitment to enter the war against Japan during a given timeframe after the defeat of Germany. Amid uncertainty regarding the necessity of an outright invasion of the Japanese home islands to bring about an end to the war in the Pacific, this pledge from the Soviets was particularly important to the US and to Great Britain. The Soviet Union went on to declare war on Japan on August 8, 1945.

On July 26, the Big Three issued the joint Potsdam Declaration, which demanded the unconditional surrender of Japan, emphasising that devastation would be wrought in the event of a full-scale invasion. The declaration further included provisions that would eliminate the militaristic government of Japan and facilitate the occupation of the home islands by Allied troops.

President Truman was advised of the successful test of the atomic bomb at the Trinity site during the Potsdam Conference and informed Stalin of the weapon's existence. Numerous issues remained unresolved at the close of the meetings, and the onset of the Cold War was becoming apparent.

Diplomats Vyacheslav Molotov of the Soviet Union, James F Byrnes of the US, and Anthony Eden of Great Britain were key figures in the discussions at Potsdam. (Creative Commons Bundesarchiv Bild via Wikimedia Commons)

HMS *VESTAL* SINKS

The Royal Navy Algerine-class minesweeper HMS *Vestal* was struck by a single Japanese Kamikaze suicide plane and seriously damaged, later to be scuttled in waters off the coast of Thailand. *Vestal* had the distinction of being the last Royal Navy vessel lost during World War Two. Twenty ratings were killed in the unfortunate action.

Just two days earlier, *Vestal*'s sister minesweeper HMS *Squirrel* sustained significant damage from a floating mine. Both stricken warships were deemed beyond repair and finally sunk by fire from Royal Navy destroyers.

The lost ships were participating in Operation Livery, supporting elements of the Eastern Fleet launching naval air strikes against Japanese installations and troop concentrations in northern Malaya. The air sorties originated off the coast of Thailand near Phuket Island in the Andaman Sea, and *Vestal* and *Squirrel* were engaged in minesweeping activities provided by the 4th and 7th Minesweeping Flotillas.

Despite more than 150 missions flown by the aircraft carrier complement of Grumman F6F Hellcat fighters that destroy more than 30 Japanese aircraft on the ground, the Royal Navy ships were still vulnerable to Kamikaze attack. Earlier in the day on July 26, a Kamikaze dived on the escort carrier HMS *Ameer* but was shot down, crashing into the sea an uncomfortable 500yds distant.

In the fading light of day, the third on station for the little minesweepers, an obsolete Mitsubishi Ki-51 bomber, known to the Allies by the codename 'Sonia', approached the tiny *Vestal*, which displaced just over 1,100 tons. When the aircraft was spotted, every gun aboard *Vestal* opened fire, including its main 4in antiaircraft weapon and quartet of 20mm guns.

Undeterred, the Kamikaze pilot pressed home his attack and dealt a savage blow to *Vestal*. Since the crippled minesweeper was off the coast of Thailand, an ally of the Japanese, there was no option to head for a friendly port. Lieutenant Charles William Porter ordered the crew to evacuate, and the survivors were transferred to the battleship HMS *Nelson*. The hulk of *Vestal* was dispatched by the destroyer HMS *Racehorse*.

The loss concluded a short service career for *Vestal*, constructed at the shipyards of Harland & Wolff in Belfast, Northern Ireland, and commissioned on February 11, 1944. The minesweeper had completed sea trials in October 1944, participated in minesweeping exercises in the estuary of the River Scheldt, and was then ordered to the Eastern Fleet in 1945.

In addition to being the last Royal Navy ship lost in World War Two, *Vestal* holds the distinction of being the only Royal Navy ship sunk by a Kamikaze during the conflict.

The guns of the destroyer HMS *Racehorse* sank the heavily damaged minesweeper *Vestal* in the Andaman Sea after the little ship was struck by a Kamikaze. (Collections of the Imperial War Museums via Wikimedia Commons)

The minesweeper HMS *Vestal* was lost to a Japanese Kamikaze attack on July 26, 1945. (Collections of the Imperial War Museums via Wikimedia Commons)

The battleship HMS *Nelson* took the survivors of the sunken HMS *Vestal* aboard during Operation Livery. (Collections of the Imperial War Museums via Wikimedia Commons)

USS *INDIANAPOLIS* SUNK BY I-58

After it completed the delivery of components for the atomic bomb 'Little Boy' to the island of Tinian in the Marianas, the heavy cruiser USS *Indianapolis* was torpedoed and sunk by the Japanese submarine I-58 in the Philippine Sea just after midnight.

Indianapolis did not sail in a zig-zag course, a prescribed procedure in waters where enemy submarines are known to operate, and two Type 95 torpedoes slammed into the starboard side of the nearly 10,000-ton warship. The first almost tore the cruiser's bow off, and the second hit amidships, rupturing fuel oil tanks and touching off secondary explosions and raging fires.

Approximately 300 sailors were killed in the initial impact, but nearly 900 of the ship's complement was thrown into the sea with only life vests or a few scattered rafts for flotation. Due to the clandestine nature of the *Indianapolis* voyage and the need to keep details of the atomic bomb secret, the route remained classified, contributing heavily to the unfortunate situation that followed.

After weighing anchor from Hunters Point Naval Shipyard in San Francisco Bay, *Indianapolis* proceeded to Pearl Harbor and then to Tinian, arriving on July 26. Captain Charles Butler McVay ordered the cruiser to Guam and then to Philippine waters to join Task Force 95. On the night of July 30, Lieutenant Commander Mochitsura Hashimoto, commander of I-58, stalked *Indianapolis* for some time before a spread of six torpedoes were fired at a distance of under 1,500yds.

Mortally wounded, *Indianapolis* sank within minutes, its stern lifting high in the air before the fatal plunge. Apparently, there was no time to

This photo depicts the forward torpedo room of the Japanese submarine I-58 at the port of Sasebo in 1946. (US Marine Corps via Wikimedia Commons)

send a distress signal. No record of the *Indianapolis* mission prompted concerns that the ship was overdue to reach its destination.

The immediate survivors of the sinking endured a harrowing ordeal at sea. Some became victims of shark attacks. Others died of wounds, dehydration, saltwater poisoning or simply let go of their flotation devices and drifted into the deep. On August 2, more than three days after the sinking, a Lockheed Ventura spotted survivors in the water. Within hours air and sea rescue operations brought 316 men to safety.

In the US Navy search for a scapegoat in the tragedy, McVay was court-martialled for failing to order the crew to abandon ship and "hazarding" the ship by failing to sail a zig-zag course. Hashimoto testified in the December 1945 proceedings that the zig-zag course would have made no difference. McVay was convicted on the second charge, but Fleet Admiral Chester Nimitz set the verdict aside and allowed the promotion of McVay to rear admiral on his retirement in 1949. McVay was the only US Navy officer court-martialled for the loss of his ship in World War Two.

In 1968, the 70-year-old McVay, burdened heavily by the loss of *Indianapolis*, committed suicide. Nearly 30 years later, the US Congress passed a resolution exonerating the officer of any wrongdoing in the loss of the ship.

The heavy cruiser USS *Indianapolis* was sunk by two torpedoes from the Japanese submarine I-58 on July 30, 1945. (US Navy via Wikimedia Commons)

The Japanese submarine I-58 at sea. The submarine fired six torpedoes at USS *Indianapolis* on July 30, 1945, and two struck home, sinking the cruiser. (Government of Japan via Wikimedia Commons)

ENOLA GAY DROPS ATOMIC BOMB ON HIROSHIMA

Enola Gay lands at Tinian in the Marianas following the mission to Hiroshima. (National Archives and Records Administration via Wikimedia Commons)

Colonel Paul W Tibbets, a 29-year-old veteran bomber pilot who participated in the first US Army Air Forces raid on Nazi-occupied Europe, revved the engines of his Boeing B-29 Superfortress, named *Enola Gay* after his mother, at North Field on the island of Tinian in the Marianas. The bomber roared down the runway into the dark sky, straining with the payload of the world's first atomic bomb – to be dropped on the Japanese city of Hiroshima, 1,570 miles away.

Tibbets commanded the 509th Bombardment Group (Composite), formed at Wendover Field, Utah, in December 1944, on the order of Manhattan Project Director General Leslie Groves, for the specific purpose of delivering the atomic bomb, if and when, the time came. With the approval of President Harry Truman, the fateful day arrived. After months of training, the 509th deployed to Tinian in May and June 1945, its B-29s modified to carry the devastating new weapon.

Four Japanese cities – Hiroshima, Nagasaki, Kyoto, and Kokura – had received little attention during the sustained American bombing campaign against the Japanese home islands, and these were chosen as potential targets for the first of two probable missions to deliver the atomic bomb. Kyoto was subsequently removed from the list due to the presence of numerous religious shrines. Hiroshima, an industrial centre with a population of 350,000, was selected as the target for the first atomic bomb.

With the atomic bomb nicknamed 'Little Boy', a gun-type weapon, aboard, Tibbets steered *Enola Gay* towards its intended target. As the B-29 arrived over Hiroshima, the presence of a single American bomber did not rouse much attention on the ground as US weather and reconnaissance planes frequent the airspace.

At 8.15am local time, the bomb bay doors of *Enola Gay* swung open and the bombardier released 'Little Boy', which detonated at an altitude of 1,900ft. The nuclear payload equivalent to 12,500 tons of TNT detonated with a blinding flash and accompanying rush of wind. A white mushroom cloud rose above Hiroshima and in seconds four square miles of the city were simply obliterated.

An estimated 80,000 people were killed swiftly, consumed in the searing heat that reached 300,000°C, most of them vaporised where they stood. Permanent shadows were later found on the pavements where a ghastly photo-like process captured the last moments of some of the dead. A short time later, radioactive black rain began to pelt the stricken city.

Captain Robert A Lewis, co-pilot of *Enola Gay*, later recalled that the bomber banked sharply away from the scene of the blast and lifted somewhat with the release of the heavy atomic bomb. Cheers gave way to an eerie silence, and Lewis whispered: "My God, what have we done?"

Casualty estimates following the Hiroshima bombing exceeded 140,000, many of those who perished suffered burns and radiation poisoning with the lingering effects of the massively destructive bomb.

Right: Before taking off for the Hiroshima mission, Colonel Paul Tibbets waves from the cockpit of *Enola Gay*, August 6, 1945. (US Army National Archives and Records Administration via Wikimedia Commons)

Hiroshima lies devastated after the atomic bomb 'Little Boy' was dropped on August 6, 1945. (US Department of Defense via Wikimedia Commons)

USS *BULLHEAD* SUNK

USS *Bullhead* is launched at Electric Boat Works in Groton, Connecticut, on July16, 1944. (US Navy via Wikimedia Commons)

On the same day that the Japanese city of Hiroshima was devastated by an atomic bomb from a US aircraft, the Balao-class submarine USS *Bullhead* became the last vessel of the US Navy lost to enemy action in World War Two.

On this fateful day, the submarine reported its passage of the Lombok Strait en route to join several other submarines to prowl the Java Sea for targets of opportunity. This was the final communication received from *Bullhead*, and on August 24, 1945, the submarine was reported as overdue and presumed lost.

For some time, the exact circumstances of the *Bullhead's* loss are unknown. However, postwar examination of Japanese records indicated that an aircraft of the Japanese Army Air Force's 73rd Independent Chutai, based near Bali, attacked and sank the submarine. The pilot of the Mitsubishi Ki-51 'Sonya' light bomber reported that he had attacked a submarine that day near the northern entrance to the Lombok Strait. The pilot asserted visual observation of two hits with depth charges followed by a gush of oil and a cloud of bubbles at the site of the attack as he lingered about ten minutes to confirm the sinking.

Analysts later concluded that surrounding mountainous terrain may well have obscured the incoming Japanese aircraft from the radar operator aboard *Bullhead*. The submarine sank with all hands, and 84 sailors lost their lives.

Bullhead was in the middle of its third war patrol at the time of its loss. Commissioned on January 4, 1944, the submarine sailed to Key West, Florida, in early January 1945 and underwent two weeks of intensive training before heading through the Panama Canal, arriving at Pearl Harbor, and then sailing on to its forward base at Guam in the Marianas Islands. During a practice dive, the submarine was nearly lost as the main induction failed to close in a timely manner due to low hydraulic pressure. Swift shifting of ballast and engaging water pumps saved the submarine from catastrophe.

During its first war patrol, *Bullhead* performed lifeguard duty, positioned in the South China Sea, to rescue downed airmen. Subsequently, the submarine bombarded Japanese positions in the Pratas Islands and narrowly escaped destruction from friendly fire off the coast of China near Macao. The submarine picked up three airmen from a downed bomber on April 16 and avoided another friendly fire incident three days later when a US bomber dropped a pair of depth charges.

Bullhead's second war patrol commenced on May 21, 1945. After nine days at sea, the submarine sank a 150-ton sailing vessel off the coast of Thailand. During bombardment of enemy cargo vessels off Java, *Bullhead* damaged or sank several small craft. The patrol ended with docking at the submarine base in Fremantle, Australia, on July 2.

The submarine's final patrol began on July 31, 1945, and it was last seen on August 4 by crewmen of a Dutch submarine during an exchange of mail in the Lombok Strait.

This memorial to the lost submarine USS *Bullhead* is located in Fremantle, Australia.
(US State Department via Wikimedia Commons)

In this July 1945 photo, the Balao-class submarine USS *Bullhead* rides on the surface of the Pacific Ocean. (US Navy via Wikimedia Commons)

SOVIET UNION DECLARES WAR ON JAPAN

Left: Red Army soldiers cross the frontier into Manchuria on August 9, 1945, a day after the Soviet declaration of war against Japan. (Creative Commons Ministry of Defence of the Russian Federation via Wikimedia Commons)

The day after the Soviet declaration, the Red Army plunged into the province of Manchuria from three directions with 1.5 million troops supported by armour and artillery. Meanwhile, amphibious landings were conducted in northern territories adjacent to the home islands of Japan. Soviet troops assaulted Sakhalin Island and overcame initial resistance to exert control there within days. Soviet forces inflicted rapid defeats on the 700,000 troops of the Kwantung Army in Manchuria, which surrendered on August 16, just hours after the formal announcement of Japanese capitulation under the terms of the Potsdam Declaration.

Aside from honouring his pledge to enter the war against Japan as soon as practical after the defeat of Nazi Germany, Stalin had several reasons for invading. The Soviet Union had long been interested in recovering territories lost to Japan during the humiliating defeat of the 1904-1905 Russo-Japanese War. Further, an extension of Soviet influence in Asia was seen as productive, while the Moscow government had long sought to dominate Manchuria and stood to gain control of the Mengjiang region of Inner Mongolia, areas of northern Korea, Sakhalin, and the Kuril Islands, stretching approximately 800 miles northeast of the northernmost Japanese home island of Hokkaido.

By August 14, Emperor Hirohito had told a meeting of his cabinet: "The military situation has changed suddenly. The Soviet Union entered the war against us. Suicide attacks cannot compete with the power of science. Therefore, there is no alternative but to accept the Potsdam terms."

Two days after the US dropped an atomic bomb on Hiroshima, Soviet Premier Josef Stalin fulfilled a promise made at the February 1945 Yalta Conference and reaffirmed in July at Potsdam, directing the government of the Soviet Union to declare war on Imperial Japan.

The declaration ends a neutrality pact between the Soviet Union and Japan that had been in effect since April 13, 1941. The pact was originally intended to be extended by five years, and its repudiation by the Soviets took the Japanese government somewhat by surprise. Many Japanese officials had not expected to contend militarily with the Soviets until at least 1946. In fact, the Japanese government had inquired about Soviet willingness to serve as an intermediary to negotiate peace terms with the US, Great Britain, and other Allied powers. This development energised the movement in Tokyo which argued for a peace to end World War Two in the Pacific as soon as possible.

Japanese soldiers surrender to the conquering Soviet Red Army during the brief fighting of August 1945. (Creative Commons Ministry of Defence of the Russian Federation via Wikimedia Commons)

Soviet troops march into the city of Harbin in the Chinese province of Manchuria after its liberation from Japanese forces. (Creative Commons Ministry of Defence of the Russian Federation via Wikimedia Commons)

BOCKSCAR DROPS ATOMIC BOMB ON NAGASAKI

The Boeing B-29 Superfortress bomber nicknamed *Bockscar*, after its primary pilot, dropped the atomic bomb 'Fat Man' on the Japanese city of Nagasaki in the second such attack in four days.

Major Charles Sweeney was the pilot for this mission, having switched planes with Captain Frederick C Bock. Bock flew Sweeney's B-29, *Great Artiste*, carrying instrumentation meant to collect data on the detonation of 'Fat Man', which was estimated at 40% more potent than 'Little Boy', that detonated above Hiroshima on August 6. 'Fat Man' was an implosion-type atomic bomb with the destructive power of 22,000 tons of TNT.

Nagasaki, a port city and shipbuilding hub on the island of Kyushu, with a population of more than 260,000 people, was also an industrial centre with two major military-related manufacturing facilities, the Mitsubishi Steel and Arms Works and the Mitsubishi-Urakami Torpedo Works, as well as other concerns that support the Japanese war effort.

Nagasaki was the third choice of the American Target Committee charged with selecting the locations for the atomic bomb missions. The original target for the second bomb, Kokura, a city of 130,000 residents that was home to major munitions and chemical weapons manufacturing facilities, was obscured by cloud cover. While Nagasaki was destined for destruction, Kokura was spared.

The second atomic bomb mission was deemed necessary due to Japanese refusal to surrender according to the terms of the Potsdam Declaration. The Americans anticipated such a response to the Hiroshima bombing and initially prepared to drop 'Fat Man' on August 11. However, anticipated bad weather, particularly the possibility of a damaging typhoon, pushed the execution date forward to August 9. Another reason for the second mission in fairly rapid succession was to convince the Japanese that the United States had a substantial stockpile of atomic weapons that it would use at will in the event of further resistance. In fact, General Leslie Groves, military

The crew of the B-29 Superfortress *Bockscar* which dropped the atomic bomb on Nagasaki poses for a photograph on August 11, 1945. (US Army via Wikimedia Commons)

leader of the Manhattan Project which produced the atomic weapons, had estimated that a third bomb would be available by August 18.

At 3.47am, Major Sweeney piloted *Bockscar* skyward from the runway at North Field on the island of Tinian in the Marianas. Cloud cover over Nagasaki and a dwindling fuel supply prompted Sweeney to momentarily consider turning towards the island of Okinawa and aborting the mission. However, a slight break in the clouds was all that was necessary for bombardier Captain Kermit Beahm to identify the target. 'Fat Man' was released over Nagasaki at 11.02am and detonated after a 43-second freefall at an altitude of 1,650ft, about two miles distant from its intended aiming point.

Surrounding hills diminished the extent of the damage, but a horrific spectacle was wrought, nevertheless. Everything within a mile of ground zero was obliterated. The Mitsubishi facilities were virtually razed, and an estimated 14,000 homes destroyed almost immediately. Although many civilians had already been evacuated from the city, 40,000 people were believed to have been killed in the initial detonation. In the weeks and months that followed, another 30,000 died of burns, radiation sickness, and other injuries. In time, the death toll attributed to the Nagasaki bombing would exceed 100,000.

Right: These before and after images of Nagasaki provide stark evidence of the destructive power of the atomic bomb dropped on August 9, 1945. (US Government via Wikimedia Commons)

Below: The harbour and port facilities at Nagasaki were photographed on August 1, 1945, days before the atomic bomb was dropped on the city. (Flt Off Bruce C Saxton/7th Air Force 11th Bomb Group Public Domain via Wikimedia Commons)

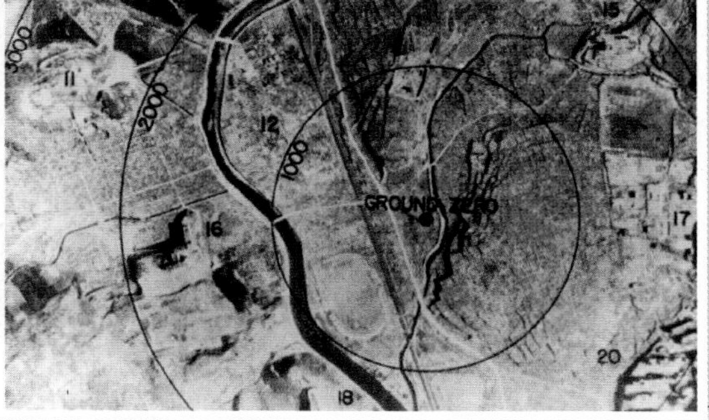

HIROHITO ISSUES SURRENDER BROADCAST

The Japanese people, for the first time in their lives, heard the 'Voice of the Crane' as their god-man Emperor Hirohito spoke to them at noon local time to announce the surrender of the Japanese Empire to the Allied nations under the terms of the Potsdam Declaration.

The address was pre-recorded the previous day, and in the first attempt the monarch's voice was less than clearly audible. He offered to complete a second recording, and this was broadcast to the people via radio following a morning announcement of the coming address. Civilians gathered near public address and radio outlets; some dressed in formal clothing.

"I have considered deeply the general trends of the world and the current situation of the Empire," stated Hirohito. "And I have decided to take extraordinary measures to bring the current state of affairs to an end. I hereby inform my loyal and devoted subjects... after four years of war, despite the valiant efforts of our land and naval forces, the diligence of our government officials, and the devoted service of our hundred million subjects, the war situation has not necessarily turned in Japan's favour. Moreover, the general trends of the world have not been advantageous to us... the enemy has begun to employ a new and cruel bomb, causing immense and indiscriminate destruction, the extent of which is beyond all estimation..."

The address, sometimes referred to as the Jewel Voice Broadcast, was delivered despite the attempt of a fanatical military faction to block the broadcast. The public statement followed a tense meeting between the emperor and his top wartime advisors the previous day. The civilian and military leaders had gathered in the underground air raid shelter of the Imperial Palace in Tokyo at 11am. Some officials argued that those who sought peace were defeatist and advocated for a final military showdown with the Allies – even to total destruction. Others profess that surrender under the terms of the Potsdam Declaration would provide the only assurance that Japan might survive and prevent the deaths of many, military and civilian, men, women, and children.

Although Hirohito rarely spoke in such meetings, his words reflected resignation to the inevitable outcome of a continued conflict. "...I cannot endure the thought of letting my people suffer any longer. A continuation of the war would bring death to tens – perhaps even hundreds – of thousands of persons. The whole nation would be reduced to ashes. How could I then carry on the wishes of my imperial ancestors? ...The time has come when we must bear the unbearable...

I swallow my tears and give my sanction to the proposal to accept the Allied proclamation on the basis outlined by the foreign minister..."

With these words, the end of World War Two in the Pacific was at hand.

Emperor Hirohito, in military dress uniform, proceeds to announce the surrender of Japan in August 1945. (Government of Japan via Wikimedia Commons)

Japanese prisoners of war on the island of Guam receive the news of their nation's surrender on August 15, 1945. (US Army via Wikimedia Commons)

Japanese civilians, some overcome with emotion, listen to Emperor Hirohito's surrender broadcast. (Government of Japan via Wikimedia Commons)

VJ DAY

Far left: Londoners, military and civilian, crowd Piccadilly Circus in celebration of victory over Japan. (Collections of the Imperial War Museums via Wikimedia Commons)

Left: In this famous VJ Day photograph a US Navy sailor kisses a woman in Times Square, Manhattan. (National Archives and Records Administration via Wikimedia Commons)

News of the unconditional surrender of Japan, ending World War Two in the Pacific, flashed around the globe and ignited spontaneous celebrations in city streets, rural areas, and aboard ships at sea. VJ Day (Victory over Japan) was celebrated worldwide.

Life magazine reported that the celebrations took place "as if joy had been rationed and saved up for three years, eight months, and seven days since Sunday, December 7, 1941…." The news marquee in New York City's Times Square repeatedly scrolled: "OFFICIAL***TRUMAN ANNOUNCES JAPANESE SURRENDER***" as the largest crowd in the history of this iconic gathered in a raucous atmosphere of merriment and relief. Military personnel and civilians take to the streets of San Francisco, where major naval installations were full of jubilant sailors and army installations brimmed with troops destined to have participated in a costly invasion of Japan that, thankfully, would not now be necessary.

In London, King George VI and Queen Elizabeth rode down The Mall to Trafalgar Square in an open carriage, while crowds filled Piccadilly Circus, Shaftesbury Avenue, and other public spaces with spontaneous toasts, singing, and dancing. From the balcony of Buckingham Palace, the King and Queen greeted the people amid their revelry. Prime Minister Clement Attlee told the British people: "Japan has today surrendered. The last of our enemies is laid low."

In Sydney, Melbourne, and Brisbane, Australia, a nation that had felt the sting of Japanese military aggression, large crowds gathered for what was initially termed VP Day (Victory in the Pacific). The *Sydney Morning Herald* newspaper estimated that crowds of 100,000 to 150,000 had gathered. In Brisbane, around 60,000 spectators viewed a parade in which 9,000 military personnel took part.

After receiving news of Japan's surrender via the Swiss government serving as intermediary, President Harry S Truman took to the radio at 7pm local time on August 14, 1945, in Washington, DC. "Arrangements are now being made for the signing of surrender terms at the earliest possible moment," Truman told his vast audience. "General Douglas MacArthur has been appointed the Supreme Allied Commander to receive the Japanese surrender. Great Britain, Russia, and China will be represented by high-ranking officers. Meantime, the Allied armed forces have been ordered to suspend offensive action. Proclamations of VJ Day must wait upon the formal signing of surrender terms by Japan…"

Despite the conditions that the President placed on the observance of VJ Day, celebrations were underway shortly after he spoke. Truman also offered: "This day is a new beginning in the history of freedom on this earth. Our global victory has come from the courage and stamina and spirit of free men and women united in determination to fight."

Formal surrender ceremonies were conducted aboard the battleship USS *Missouri* in Tokyo Bay on September 2, 1945. While many nations continued to observe August 15 as VJ Day, the signing date has also remained significant in the history of World War Two.

A tumultuous crowd celebrates VJ Day in Times Square, New York City. (Library of Congress via Wikimedia Commons)

TRIAL OF TRAITOR VIDKUN QUISLING BEGINS

Far left: Vidkun, a Norwegian Nazi collaborator, was shot by firing squad in 1945. To this day his name is synonymous with 'traitor'. (National Archives of Norway via Wikimedia Commons)

Left: Vidkun Quisling (left) while imprisoned at Akershus Fortress in 1945. (National Archives of Norway via Wikimedia Commons)

Below: Norwegian Nazi sympathiser Vidkun Quisling delivers a speech during a rally of the far right in Norway. (National Archives of Norway via Wikimedia Commons)

The trial of Norwegian Nazi and traitor Vidkun Quisling got underway in Olso. A former politician and army officer, Quisling was convicted of high treason, murder, and crimes against the nation, and during the three-week proceedings the evidence against him was substantial.

The guilty verdict was rendered on September 10, 1945, and Quisling was shot by firing squad on October 24, at the Akershus Fortress in the Norwegian capital city. At least 37 other individuals were convicted of treason and collaboration with the Germans during the prewar years and through World War Two. They were also executed.

In the early 1930s, Quisling had founded the pro-Nazi Fascist National Union Party, and prior to the German invasion of Norway in April 1940, he provided aid and support to the Nazis while soon attempting a coup d'etat to seize power in the country.

In February 1942, Quisling formed a government subservient to the Nazis. He remained in power as minister president along with his German overseer, Josef Terboven, officially titled civilian administrator. The puppet government assisted the Nazis in identifying, rounding up, and deporting Norwegian Jews to concentration camps in other occupied territories, leading to the deaths of thousands. Quisling travelled to Germany to meet with Adolf Hitler on several occasions.

After the collapse of the Nazi regime, Quisling was arrested on May 9, 1945, and imprisoned first in the Oslo police station before being transferred to Akershus Fortress to stand trial. Upon his arrest, Quisling commented: "I know that the Norwegian people have sentenced me to death, and that the easiest course for me would be to take my own life. But I want to let history reach its own verdict. Believe me, in ten years' time I will have become another Saint Olaf."

Observers noted that Quisling had once been arrogant and ruthless but that his demeanour had changed to one of apparent fear and nervousness as he entered the courtroom to beg for his life. He requested to be treated in the same manner as others of his pro-Nazi puppet regime but hoped to avoid the status of a common criminal.

A legal appeal failed to change the verdict and sentence, and at 2.40pm on October 24, Quisling was executed. Just before the fatal shots were fired, he muttered in a trembling voice: "I am convicted unfairly and I die innocent."

The name Quisling lives on in infamy and is synonymous with the word traitor.

MACARTHUR ASSUMES GOVERNMENT IN TOKYO

General Douglas MacArthur assumed control of military forces occupying the defeated nation of Japan and took the reins of government with sweeping authority. Designated Supreme Commander of the Allied Powers, his administration lasted until 1952, literally reshaping Japan through military, political, economic, and social initiatives.

MacArthur met Japanese Emperor Hirohito, allowed to remain on the Chrysanthemum Throne under the terms of the peace that ended World War Two in the Pacific, for the first time on September 27, 1945. Although some observers had called for the prosecution of Hirohito as a war criminal, MacArthur favoured retaining the emperor as the monarch of the Japanese people to reduce the prospect of civil unrest and facilitate the implementation of extensive reforms in the island nation. In turn, Hirohito renounced his perceived divinity before the public and acquiesced to the role of figurehead.

MacArthur turned his immediate attention to the apprehension and prosecution of suspected Japanese war criminals. He established the first International Military Tribunal in the Far East, and 28 suspected war criminals were placed on trial in Tokyo beginning in April 1946 and concluding November 12, 1948. MacArthur's administration further dismantled the Japanese military apparatus and forbade former officers from participating in leadership positions in the new government. The Japanese economy was recast into a free-market capitalist system amid the breakup of many industrial conglomerates whose leaders had supported the waging of aggressive war since the early 1930s. The administration also enacted land reform to provide relief for tenant farmers, long oppressed by wealthy landowners.

By 1947, a new constitution was introduced in Japan. Based on the US Constitution, the document vested more authority in a legislative form of government and reduced the influence of the emperor to a merely symbolic post-war role. The rights of women were also extended. The new Japanese government was required to renounce war, and the nation's armed forces were allowed to reconstitute in sufficient strength for defensive purposes only.

Even with the outbreak of the Korean War in 1950 and MacArthur's appointment to command the United Nations forces, reforms continued in Japan as efforts to secure the economic and political future of the country against Communist expansion emerged as a priority. Today, the Japanese people remember MacArthur both as an authoritative figure who mandated great change and as the benefactor of the defeated country who ushered in needed reforms and set the stage for a remarkable resurgence of Japanese economic growth, a significant development of the latter half of the 20th century.

Left: General Douglas MacArthur meets Japanese Emperor Hirohito in Tokyo, September 1945. (US Army via Wikimedia Commons)

Right: General Douglas MacArthur, leader of the American forces occupying Japan, strikes a pose in 1945. (US Army via Wikimedia Commons)

Below: Damage from American bombs is visible in this photo of a busy Tokyo street taken during the occupation in 1946. (Government of Japan via Wikimedia Commons)

THE DESTINATION FOR
HISTORIC & MILITARY ENTHUSIASTS

Visit us today and discover all our publications

KEY Publishing

FlyPast is internationally regarded as the magazine for aviation history and heritage.

Aeroplane is still providing the best aviation coverage around, with focus on iconic military aircraft from the 1930s to the 1960s.

and subscribe to your favourite magazine...
/collections/subscriptions

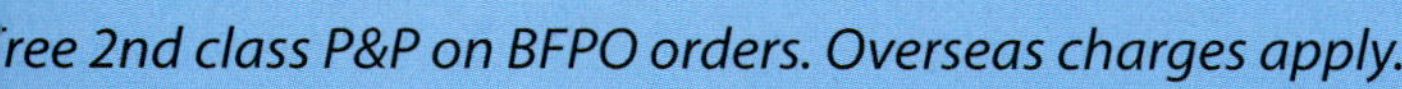

Free 2nd class P&P on BFPO orders. Overseas charges apply.

STATE OF WAR

Mushroom clouds rise over the Japanese cities of Hiroshima (left) and Nagasaki in August 1945. (US Department of Energy via Wikimedia Commons)

The end of the Third Reich came with a resounding Allied victory, but the simple surrender of the Nazi armed forces in a schoolhouse in Reims, France, is insufficient for Soviet Premier Josef Stalin. That particular surrender occurred in the West, and it is the Soviet military and civilian population that had suffered most grievously in the final victory of World War Two in Europe.

Stalin saw the symbolism and the closure in a second Nazi surrender, this time in Berlin on May 8, 1945, a day later than the capitulation in France. Ironically, it was indeed the Soviets who had lost 20 million people in the conflagration of World War Two on the Eastern Front. Therefore, Premier Stalin was perhaps justified in his desire for a repeat

Soviet General Ivan Susloparov signs the Nazi surrender document at Reims, France, but another ceremony takes place a day later in Berlin. (National Museum of the US Navy via Wikimedia Commons)

US troops take cover from the blast of an artillery shell fired into a cave which conceals a Japanese strongpoint on Okinawa. (US Government via Wikimedia Commons)

performance from the vanquished. General Dwight D Eisenhower, Supreme Commander of Allied Forces in Western Europe, agrees. Yet, there is irony in the Berlin ceremonies. The Soviets and the Nazis had been erstwhile partners just a few years earlier, signatories to a non-aggression pact with a secret protocol that specified the division of Poland between their two conquering armies.

By now, the Soviets had destroyed the defenders of their sworn enemy's capital and stood with the Red Army in control of vast territory, including the venerable cities of old eastern Europe. In the immediate aftermath of World War Two on the continent lay the seeds of the Cold War, the distrust, the promises made and then broken, and the half-century of intrigue, political posturing, and proxy wars to follow.

Prisoners cheer the arrival of American soldiers at the Dachau concentration camp. Such scenes were repeated through the spring of 1945. (US Government via Wikimedia Commons)

At this time, however, there were other urgent issues to be considered. The leaders of the victorious Allies met at Potsdam in the suburbs of Berlin to continue their discussion on the shape of the post-war world, particularly the issue of self-determination for countries in eastern Europe freed from the grip of the Nazis. US President Franklin D Roosevelt was dead, and the nation continued in mourning as Vice President Harry S Truman was sworn in and subsequently took his place in the proceedings. Prime Minister Winston Churchill also attended, but he was replaced amid the discussions by Clement Attlee, the man of the Labour Party, following the shock of the July general elections in Britain. The wily, suspicious Stalin, however, is a constant.

The Allied leaders conferred on the disposition of refugees, hundreds of thousands removed from their homes during the Nazi rampage, and others seeded in the eastern territories as German settlers in newly conquered land fulfilling the notion of Nazi Lebensraum (Living Space), from the frontier of the Reich to the Russian steps and beyond. Prisoners of war needed to be repatriated, while civilian refugees were wholly dependent on the victors for shelter and to fend off the spectre of starvation.

Allied troops uncovered the unspeakable horrors of the death camps across Germany and occupied territories. The matter of war criminal pursuit, arrest, and prosecution became urgent. The Allied authorities hunted down many former Nazi officials suspected of crimes against humanity. Some committed suicide prior to being arrested. Others sought to blend in with the masses of people heading home – if there is a home – or just plodding towards an uncertain future. Reichsmarschall Hermann Göring arranged to give himself up, while Reichsführer SS Heinrich Himmler was discovered in a dirty enlisted soldier's uniform as he tried to escape detection. The ruse failed and his final act was suicide by ingesting cyanide poison as a British doctor looks on, powerless to stop him. In time, Göring would also cheat the hangman. However, the International Military Tribunal at Nuremberg loomed first for Göring and 23 other top Nazis.

Across the world, great tracts of Japanese cities became veritable funeral pyres in relentless American firebombing raids. Operation Meetinghouse burnt the heart out of Tokyo as fires raged on the night of March 9.

The battle for Okinawa, on the doorstep of the Japanese home islands, raged for 82 days, finally ending in late June after thousands of casualties were sustained in the bloodiest battle of the war in the Pacific. Scores of US Marines and Army troops fought and died just to gain a few yards on the bitterly contested island as many of the Japanese defenders fought to the end. The nicknames of previously innocuous terrain features resonate through the annals of American military history: Sugar Loaf, Half Moon, Horseshoe, Conical Hill, and more.

Offshore, the US Navy's Fifth Fleet (operationally renamed the Third Fleet when Admiral William F 'Bull' Halsey rotated to command in relief of Admiral Raymond A Spruance in late May) earnt the nickname 'fleet that came to stay', enduring countless enemy attacks from Kamikaze suicide planes. Some sailors died amid the many strikes. Others were grievously wounded. Still others could not cope in this crucible of cruel war. One sailor stood up at his antiaircraft gun mount and shouted: "It's hot today!" He then leapt into the sea and disappeared. As the full realisation of the 'butcher's bill' at Okinawa stared them in the face, Allied war planners considered an invasion of the Japanese home islands with increasing dread.

Then, on August 6, the atomic bomb devastated Hiroshima. On the 9th a second atomic bomb wreaked destruction on Nagasaki. At long last, Emperor Hirohito would hear no more from those advisors who demanded a fight to the death – the death of the entire Japanese nation and her people. He agreed to the terms of unconditional surrender issued in the Potsdam Declaration and made a stunning radio broadcast to his subjects. The war in the Pacific ended with jubilant celebration across the globe; however, beyond the unbridled joy of VJ Day, the cost of victory was staggering. A colossal effort would now be devoted to winning the peace.

This photo of Hermann Göring was taken shortly after his capture. His medals and rank insignia were stripped from him by the Allied captors. (US Government via Wikimedia Commons)

Allied leaders and associates crowd into a room during the Potsdam Conference while the media document the proceedings. (National Museum of the US Navy via Wikimedia Commons)

JAPANESE FORMAL SURRENDER IN TOKYO BAY

Hundreds of warships of the US Pacific Fleet and the Royal Navy Pacific Fleet crowded Tokyo Bay, waves of aircraft flew overhead, newsreel cameras clicked, and ordinary sailors strained for a view of the proceedings. On Sunday, September 2, 1945, Imperial Japan, its delegates in formal civilian attire and military uniform, surrendered unconditionally to the Allied forces, ending World War Two in the Pacific.

Three days earlier, General Douglas MacArthur's personal C-54 Douglas Skymaster transport plane, nicknamed '*Bataan*', touched down at Atsugi air base near Tokyo at 2.19pm. MacArthur had been named Supreme Commander of the Allied Powers and was to lead the postwar administration and occupation of Japan. He was also to preside over the formal Japanese surrender ceremonies aboard the battleship USS *Missouri*.

The location chosen for the Japanese surrender was an artful compromise between the armed forces with a nod to the home state of President Harry S Truman. The US chief executive was a native of Missouri, which explained the choice of that particular warship. The US Navy and Marine Corps bore a heavy weight in prosecuting the Pacific War, and the US Army and Army Air Forces also contributed mightily. In order to avoid any slight, the surrender took place aboard a battleship with numerous senior naval officers present, while an army general served as master of ceremonies and many high-ranking army officers took their place on the Missouri's deck.

The host of photographers and reporters began to arrive around 7.30am on this cool, grey morning. The destroyers came alongside in succession to deliver their cargoes of officers and dignitaries. Fleet Admiral Chester W Nimitz, Commander-in-Chief of Allied forces in the Pacific, arrived at 8.05am, and General MacArthur was aboard just a few minutes later.

MacArthur, unsmiling and businesslike, greeted Nimitz and Admiral William F 'Bull' Halsey, commander of the US Third Fleet, remarking: "It's grand to have so many of my colleagues from the shoestring days here at the end of the road." MacArthur led a delegation of 89 American officers, including 34 admirals, and 39 generals. Also present were 43 high-ranking officers from eight Allied nations.

The Japanese delegation arrives aboard the battleship USS *Missouri* in Tokyo Bay, September 2, 1945. (US Army Signal Corps via Wikimedia Commons)

Japanese Foreign Minister Mamoru Shigemitsu signs the surrender document as US General Richard Sutherland looks on. (US Army Signal Corps via Wikimedia Commons)

Battleships of the US Navy and the Royal Navy Pacific Fleet ride at anchor in Tokyo Bay with Mount Fuji in the background. (US Navy via Wikimedia Commons)

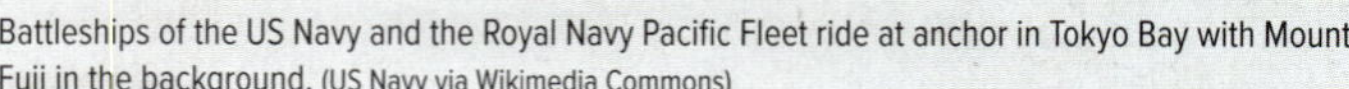

At 8.56am, the 11 representatives of the Japanese government came alongside *Missouri* aboard the destroyer USS *Lansdowne*. Foreign Minister Mamoru Shigemitsu, crippled since an assassin's bomb had blown part of his left leg off years earlier in Shanghai, led the party aboard with his painful gait. The surrender documents were laid across the green felt top of an ordinary mess hall table, spread out discreetly to cover its indelible coffee stains.

The proceedings began at 9.02am as MacArthur, Nimitz, and Halsey strode briskly across the battleship's teak deck then stood rigidly. Toshikazu Kase, a high-ranking member of the Japanese Foreign Ministry later remarked: "We waited a few minutes, standing in the public gaze like penitent schoolboys awaiting the dreaded schoolmaster. A million eyes seemed to beat on us like arrows barbed with fire. I felt them sink into my body with a sharp physical pain."

After the *Missouri*'s chaplain delivered a brief prayer and a recording of the US national anthem was played over the battleship's public address system, MacArthur stepped forward and intoned: "We are gathered here, representatives of the major warring powers, to conclude a solemn agreement whereby peace may be restored... It is my earnest hope, indeed the hope of all mankind, that from this solemn occasion a better world shall emerge out of the blood and carnage of the past, a world founded upon faith and understanding, a world dedicated to the dignity of man and the fulfilment of his most cherished wish for freedom, tolerance, and justice."

Shigemitsu was invited to sign the instrument of surrender but became confused, and MacArthur ordered his chief of staff General Richard K Sutherland to assist. He croaked: "Sutherland, show him where to sign." Japanese Army Chief of Staff General Yoshijiro Umezu followed.

MacArthur used three pens to sign for the Allied powers. The first of these was handed to General Jonathan M Wainwright, who surrendered in the Philippines in the spring of 1942 and endured captivity. The second was presented to General Arthur Percival, who

General Douglas MacArthur signs the surrender document ending World War Two in the Pacific. (US Navy via Wikimedia Commons)

surrendered the British and Commonwealth garrison in Singapore that same year and also became a prisoner of the Japanese. MacArthur placed the third pen in his pocket, intending it as a gift for his wife, Jean, and son, Arthur, then in the Philippine capital of Manila.

Admiral Nimitz stepped forward to sign for the United States, and Admiral Bruce Fraser signed as the representative of Great Britain. Other Allied military officers signed for their respective countries. All the while, Admiral Halsey appeared to be mumbling under his breath. A reporter spotted this and quipped that the salty veteran was "apparently still cussin' the enemy."

The entire ceremony required only 23 minutes, start to finish. At 9.25am, General MacArthur concluded with the statement: "Let us pray that peace now be restored to the world, and that God will preserve it always. These proceedings are now closed."

With Wainwright and Percival by his side, MacArthur walked towards Admiral Halsey's cabin. He did not offer even a passing glance

Surrounded by Allied officers, General Douglas MacArthur addresses the gathering aboard the battleship USS *Missouri*, September 2, 1945. (US Navy via Wikimedia Commons)

Waves of Allied fighters and bombers fly above Tokyo Bay with USS Missouri anchored in the foreground. (US Navy via Wikimedia Commons)

at the Japanese delegates. Putting his arm around Halsey, he asked: "Bill, where in the hell are those airplanes?"

Moments later, 1,900 Allied fighter and bomber aircraft roared overhead in salute. A young seaman noticed one of the Japanese delegates looking skyward and concluded: "You could see him looking up and smiling. I guess he knew they meant business."

The most catastrophic armed conflict in the history of human civilisation was finally over. Estimates of the dead alone approached 85 million, and approximately 30% of these occurred in the Pacific theatre.

BERLIN VICTORY PARADE

Often remembered as the "forgotten parade" because its size was overshadowed by that of a British commemoration just weeks earlier, the four major Allied powers that achieved victory over the Nazis staged another victory parade through the streets of Berlin.

The United States, Soviet Union, Great Britain, and France participated in the event, which was proposed by the Soviets and came a few weeks after a large victory parade in Moscow. Although Red Army Marshal Georgy Zhukov and French General Marie-Pierre Koenig were present, General Dwight Eisenhower, Supreme Commander of Allied Forces in Western Europe, did not attend, sending General George S Patton, Jr, commander of the US Third Army, in his stead. British Field Marshal Bernard Montgomery, commander of 21st Army Group, also declined and was represented by General Brian Robertson, his chief of staff and Deputy Military Governor of the British Occupation Zone. Newly elected British Prime Minister Clement Attlee was also in attendance.

Among the participating units were the British 7th Armoured Division, the famed 'Desert Rats' of the North Africa and European campaigns, the US Army's 16th Mechanized Cavalry Group, and the French 1st Armoured Division. The Red Army chose the occasion to unveil its new IS-3 heavy tank. Although the armoured vehicle had reached frontline units after the Nazi surrender and saw no action during World War Two, its debut in Berlin made a bold statement on behalf of the strength of the Soviet armed forces. More than 50 Red Army tanks of the 2nd Guards Tank Army took part in the parade.

The primary route of the parade was along the Charlottenburger Chausee west of the Brandenburg Gate and near the site of the bitter battle for the Reichstag. The parade was held in conjunction with the Potsdam Conference convened in a Berlin suburb, and as many as 6,000 Allied soldiers take part. The event was further viewed by many as an observance of VJ Day, the end of World War Two in the Pacific, five days after the formal Japanese surrender.

Initially, the Soviets had planned for a larger number of troops but decided later to limit the participation. In the event, about 2,000 Red Army soldiers marched, while the British, American, and French contingents were about half that size.

British Army self-propelled Sexton guns participate in the September 7, 1945, Berlin Victory Parade. (Collections of the Imperial War Museums via Wikimedia Commons)

Prior to the start of the parade, Marshal Zhukov was driven to the head of the gathering in a US-built open-top Packard Twelve. The Soviet 248th Infantry Division led, followed by the French 2nd Infantry Division, the British 131st Infantry Brigade, and the US 82nd Airborne Division with the armoured formations following behind.

The entire parade review was completed in about two hours.

The French tricolour flies from the top of the 19th century Prussian Victory Column in Berlin during the September 7, 1945, victory parade. (ECPAD Archives Government of France via Wikimedia Commons)

Brand new Soviet IS-3 heavy tanks rumble down the Charlottenburger Chausee in Berlin on September 7, 1945. (Collections of the Imperial War Museums via Wikimedia Commons)

FORMER PRIME MINISTER TOJO ATTEMPTS SUICIDE

In an effort to avoid trial for war crimes, former Japanese Prime Minister Hideki Tojo, nicknamed 'The Razor', fired a bullet into his stomach during a botched suicide attempt. Tojo has been a prime mover in the emergence of Japanese imperialism and military aggression in Asia and the Pacific, and had risen to prominence while serving as Vice Minister of War and supporting Japan's entry into the Axis Tripartite Pact of 1940.

Tojo expanded his influence in the Japanese government and clashed with more moderate officials, forcing Prime Minister Prince Fumimaro Konoye to resign in October 1940 and assuming the post himself while consolidating his power as minister of the army, minister of war, and minister of commerce and industry. Tojo supported the bombing of the US Pacific Fleet and installations at Pearl Harbor in December 1941, and announced the Japanese war aim of establishing the "Greater East Asia Co-Prosperity Sphere". He coerced or persuaded many senior military officers and government officials to follow him towards war with the United States, Great Britain and its Commonwealth, and other European countries.

Although Japanese forces were successful early in World War Two in the Pacific, by early 1943 substantial setbacks had occurred. As the fortunes of war turned against Japan, Tojo's responsibility for leading the nation towards catastrophe was difficult to deny. He lost the confidence of Emperor Hirohito by the autumn of that year as the Jushin (Senior Statesmen), faction organised against him, pointing to the numerous failures under his leadership. After the Marianas Islands had fallen to the Americans in the summer of 1944, Tojo and his entire cabinet resigned on July 18, ending his 33-month tenure as virtual dictator of the country's war plans and foreign policy.

Following the end of the war in the Pacific, Tojo was arrested on September 8, 1945. Three days later, while under guard at his home 12 miles outside the city of Tokyo, he was informed that charges of war crimes against him would be filed shortly. He shot himself once in the stomach with a .32-calibre pistol at 4.21pm. He lost consciousness for more than 20 minutes, but after reviving gasps, said: "I wanted to die by the sword, but the pistol had to do. I assume the responsibility for the war. Banzai!"

Within hours of the clumsy shooting, Tojo was treated at the US Army's 98th Evacuation Hospital in Yokohama. He received several lifesaving transfusions of blood and survived to be transferred to Sugamo Prison in Tokyo. He stood trial there before the International Military Tribunal for the Far East, which convened in April 1946. Convicted and sentenced to death, he was hanged on December 23, 1948.

Disgraced former Japanese Prime Minister Hideki Tojo attempted suicide on September 11, 1945. (Government of Japan via Wikimedia Commons)

Tojo testifies during his war crimes trial in Tokyo. He was convicted, sentenced to death, and hanged in December 1948. (US Government via Wikimedia Commons)

Hideki Tojo lies unconscious in a chair in his study after a self-inflicted gunshot wound. (US Government via Wikimedia Commons)

LORD HAW HAW SENTENCED TO DEATH

The odious William Joyce, popularly known as Lord Haw Haw, was sentenced to death in Number One Court at the Old Bailey in London for the crime of treason. Joyce was one of a handful of British citizens who openly sympathised with Hitler and the Nazi regime in Germany. He was a virulent anti-Semite, who had fled, along with his wife, to Germany in the days before the outbreak of World War Two.

By mid-September 1939, Joyce had taken a job with the German Reich Ministry of Public Enlightenment and Propaganda, making radio broadcasts from the Berlin-Charlottenburg area. The diatribe was aimed directly at undermining the morale and fighting spirit of the British people, and it is said virtually every Briton recognised the pompous public radio voice of the turncoat propagandist. Although his wartime broadcasts created a sensation for a brief period, Joyce earned the nickname 'Lord Haw Haw', and his drivel was lampooned across Britain.

The broadcasts began with a braying style: "This is Germany calling, Germany calling…" and Joyce also authored a small book titled *Twilight Over England* espousing his anti-Semitic claptrap. He was heard on the airwaves to have spouted the "necessity of liquidating all Jews everywhere".

By 1945, as the demise of the Third Reich was imminent, Joyce attempted to flee the British retribution that was sure to come. Harebrained schemes of quietly escaping to neutral Sweden via Denmark

British soldiers pose with the prisoner Lord Haw Haw after the propagandist traitor's arrest on May 28, 1945. (Government of Great Britain via Wikimedia Commons)

and evacuation aboard a U-boat that would then deposit him safely on the west coast of Ireland came to nothing. Joyce was captured outside Flensburg, Germany, on May 28, 1945, after speaking first in French and then English, his distinctive accent betraying his identity. He had not been required to speak but gave himself away. Joyce made a second mistake when he reached for his pocket, and a British officer promptly shot him in the buttock.

Joyce stood trial in September 1945, charged with three counts of treason. Two of these were dismissed due to his attorney's assertion that Joyce was an American citizen and therefore not a subject of the crown. His father had been American, and his British mother was a naturalised citizen of the US.

However, the third count focused on Joyce's (fraudulently obtained) British passport for proof that the defendant relied on the protection of His Majesty's government and therefore owed allegiance to Great Britain.

After sentencing, William Joyce was incarcerated in Wandsworth Prison and hanged on the morning of January 3, 1946.

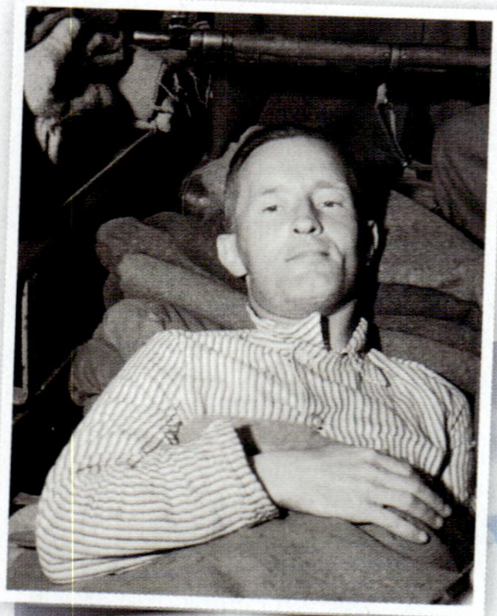

Left: After being captured and wounded, William Joyce awaits transfer to a British Army hospital. (Government of Great Britain via Wikimedia Commons)

Below: Convicted of treason, Lord Haw Haw was executed at Wandsworth Prison in January 1946. (Creative Commons Front block, Wandsworth Prison by Robin Webster via Wikimedia Commons)

PATTON RELIEVED OF THIRD ARMY COMMAND

Outspoken General George S Patton Jr was relieved of command of the US Third Army on October 2, 1945. (Creative Commons National Portrait Gallery via Wikimedia Commons)

Outspoken and controversial, General George S Patton Jr, was relieved of command of the US Third Army, which has compiled an impressive combat record under his leadership during World War Two in Europe. The Third Army has executed a brilliant campaign across France, relieved the besieged garrison of Bastogne, Belgium, during the Battle of the Bulge, and inflicted heavy casualties on the Nazi enemy. However, it was characteristically Patton's own caustic tongue that results in his transfer to command the Fifteenth Army at Bad Nauheim, 24 miles north of Frankfurt, Germany, which was writing a history of the war.

Only his friendship with General Dwight D Eisenhower, Supreme Commander of Allied Forces in Western Europe, and the need for seasoned combat leadership saved Patton's career following two instances of slapping shellshocked soldiers in Sicily in 1943. However, in April 1944, unaware that reporters were covering the event, he told a gathering in Knutsford, Cheshire: "It is the evident destiny of the British and Americans, and of course, the Russians, to rule the world."

Eisenhower was livid and rebuked Patton with the admonition that another such comment would result in his immediate relief from command.

Nevertheless, the flamboyant Patton continued a series of self-inflicted wounds. After criticizing Jewish influence in the shaping of the post-war peace and interfering with his administration as military governor of Bavaria, the general told General Joseph McNarney, one of Eisenhower's deputies, that the Russians could not be trusted. He ranted: "Hell, we are going to have to fight them sooner or later. Why not do it now while our army is intact and we can have their hind end kicked back into Russia in three months?"

The final incident occurred at Bad Tolz, south of Munich, on September 22, 1945, when Patton told a gathering of reporters: "In supervising the functioning of the Bavarian government, which is my mission, the first thing that happened was that the outs accused the ins of being Nazis. Now, more than half the German people were Nazis, and we would be in a hell of a fix if we removed all Nazi party members from office. The way I see it, this Nazi question is very much like a Democratic and Republican election fight. To get things done in Bavaria, after the complete disorganisation and disruption of four years of war, we had to compromise with the Devil a little."

On September 30, Eisenhower's Chief of Staff, General Walter Bedell Smith, informs Patton that he is being relieved. The ensuing ceremonial handover of the Third Army to General Lucian Truscott was completed in just a few minutes, and Patton boarded the train for Bad Nauheim after commenting: "All good things must come to an end. The best thing that has ever happened to me thus far is the honour and privilege of having commanded the Third Army..."

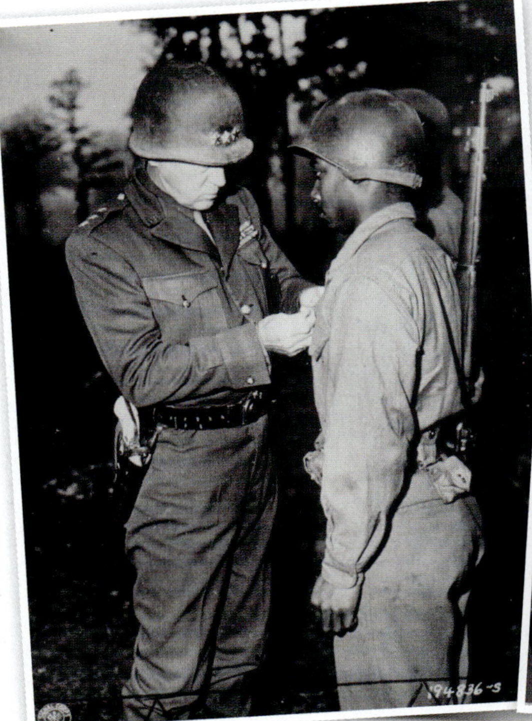

Below left: General Patton presents the Silver Star Medal to Private Ernest Jenkins in October 1944. (National Archives and Records Administration via Wikimedia Commons)

Below right: Generals Patton (left) and Eisenhower confer during the North Africa Campaign in Tunisia, 1943. (US Army via Wikimedia Commons)

TRIAL OF PIERRE LAVAL BEGINS IN PARIS

The trial of pro-Nazi traitor and one-time head of the collaborationist government of Vichy, France, Pierre Laval began in Paris. Although he started his political career as a socialist, Laval turned towards the right during the 1930s while serving twice as prime minister and as foreign minister of France prior to the outbreak of World War Two.

Laval later became the lieutenant of Marshal Philippe Pétain, head of the Nazi puppet state of Vichy, after Pétain chose the path of collaboration rather than resistance like his protégé, General Charles de Gaulle. Laval supported the peace initiative with the invading Germans in 1940, which lead to the capitulation of France, and he served in numerous capacities in the Vichy government, including vice president of the council of ministers and head of the puppet state. When Pétain fired him in 1940 for carrying on separate discussions with the German government, the Nazis demanded his reinstatement.

By April 1942, the 85-year-old Pétain handed over the reins of Vichy's government to Laval. who pursued an openly collaborationist policy. He co-operated in the Nazi round-up and deportation of French Jews to concentration camps and assisted in furnishing forced labourers sent to work in the factories of the Third Reich. Although he and Pétain refused to commit Vichy France fully to direct fighting against the Allies, Laval became one of the world's best known and most villainous Nazi collaborators.

With the ongoing Allied liberation of France in 1944, Laval was forced to flee eastward to Germany. However, he was arrested by his former benefactors. Although he managed to escape to Spain, he was thrown out of the country by Generalissimo Francisco Franco, the Fascist Spanish leader, in an attempt to curry favour with the Allies. Laval was handed over to American authorities upon arriving at Hörsching Airport in Linz, Austria, on July 31, 1945. Extradited to France, his trial on charges of treason and collaboration with the Nazis before the High Court of Justice concluded in less than a week. He

Pierre Laval shouts during courtroom proceedings at his trial in Paris in 1945. He is convicted of treason and collaboration with the Nazis, and shot by firing squad. (European Union Public Domain via Wikimedia Commons)

was absent from the courtroom when the guilty verdict and sentence of death were pronounced.

Laval ingested poison in a failed attempt at suicide, but sufficiently recovered for his execution. He was shot by a firing squad at Fresnes Prison outside Paris on October 15, 1945.

Left: Leaders of the government of Vichy France, Marshal Philippe Pétain (left) and Pierre Laval are shown in 1942. (European Union Public Domain via Wikimedia Commons)

Below: Vichy French leader and Nazi collaborationist Pierre Laval was convicted of treason and shot. (Agence de presse Meurisse via Wikimedia Commons)

NUREMBERG TRIBUNAL ISSUES FORMAL CHARGES

The International Military Tribunal at Nuremberg, Germany, issued formal charges against 24 top Nazis related to four specifications: crimes against peace, conspiracy to commit crimes against peace, war crimes and crimes against humanity. The charge of crimes against humanity was described by the tribunal as "murder, extermination, enslavement, deportation or persecutions on political, racial or religious grounds".

The tribunal's presiding judge was Lord Justice Geoffrey Lawrence of Great Britain, while other members of the tribunal included Associate Justice of the Supreme Court Robert Jackson of the United States, Sir Hartley Shawcross of Great Britain, Francois de Menthon of France and Roman A Rudenko of the Soviet Union. The city of Nuremberg was chosen because of its significance in the Nazi past that would serve as evidence of the end of the 12-year Third Reich reign of terror. The proceedings were scheduled to begin in the city's Palace of Justice on November 20, 1945.

The unprecedented international court was an outgrowth of the recognition by the Allied powers that atrocities had been committed by the Nazi regime as evidenced during the Moscow Conference of October 1943. During that meeting, President Franklin D Roosevelt, Prime Minister Winston Churchill and Soviet Premier Joseph Stalin signed the Declaration of Atrocities, which read in part: "The United Kingdom, the United States and the Soviet Union have received from many quarters evidence of atrocities, massacres and cold-blooded mass executions perpetrated by Hitlerite forces in many countries they have overrun... Those German officers and men and members of the Nazi party who have been responsible for or have taken a consenting part in the above atrocities, massacres and executions will be sent back to the countries in which their abominable deeds were done in order that they may be judged and punished according to the laws of these liberated countries and of free governments which will be erected therein...."

Among the indicted Nazi leaders were Reichsmarschall Hermann Göring, head of the Luftwaffe and widely known as the second most powerful of Hitler's henchmen; former Deputy Führer Rudolf Hess; Foreign Minister Joachim von Ribbentrop; Field Marshal Wilhelm Keitel, Chief of the German High Command; Colonel General Alfred Jodl, German High Command Chief of Operations; Hans Frank, Governor General of Occupied Poland; Ernst Kaltenbrunner, head of the Reich Main Security Office; Baldur von Schirach, head of the Hitler Youth; Julius Streicher, publisher of the anti-Semitic newspaper *Der Stürmer*; Albert Speer, Minister of Armaments and War Production; and several others.

Those who escaped prosecution included Hitler, Reichsführer SS Heinrich Himmler and Propaganda Minister Josef Goebbels, each having committed suicide. The day before the trials begin, Robert Ley, chief of the Nazi Labour Front, committed suicide too. Martin Bormann, Hitler's personal secretary, was tried in absentia.

Above: The Palace of Justice in Nuremberg, Germany, is shown in this aerial photograph from November 1945. (US Army via Wikimedia Commons)

Right: US Army clerks work amid a mountain of evidence compiled for the prosecution of the indicted Nazi leaders at Nuremberg. (US Army via Wikimedia Commons)

Below: The formal indictments of top Nazis are presented during a session of the International Military Tribunal at Nuremberg, October 18, 1945. (US Army via Wikimedia Commons)

UNITED NATIONS CHARTER EFFECTIVE

After years of theorising, discussions and negotiations, the charter of the newly-organised United Nations became effective. Previously signed by representatives of 50 nations on June 26, 1945, the document came into force after being ratified by the five permanent members of the body's Security Council – the United Kingdom, the United States, the Soviet Union, France and China.

The charter established the organisation's formal structure, framework of the system and procedures and six primary bodies encompassed. These included the Security Council, General Assembly, International Court of Justice, Secretariat, Economic and Social Council and the Trusteeship Council. In the wake of the failure of its predecessor, the League of Nations, the United Nations revived a pledge to eliminate armed warfare and raise the standard of living for people across the globe along with their health while addressing economic and social issues that were pervasive in the post-World War Two period.

The preamble to the charter was followed by 111 articles that were grouped into 19 chapters. After describing the structure and purpose of the international organisation, it devoted nine chapters to the anticipated enforcement capabilities that had been approved. These included the ability to investigate and mediate disputes, impose economic, diplomatic and military sanctions, and to deploy troops under the United Nations banner. Interestingly, the Trusteeship Council was dedicated to the emerging phenomenon of decolonisation, the dismantling of colonial empires, that had gained energy since the end of the war.

The summer conference in San Francisco had been the largest such gathering of nations in history in all likelihood with a total of 850 international delegates who, with their advisers and support staffs, brought the grand total of participants to about 3,500. Following plenary sessions and committee meetings conducted to finalise the proposed draft for full approval, the document was signed in the city's Veterans' Memorial Hall.

The United States Senate ratified the charter by a vote of 89-2, while the British Foreign Office approved for the United Kingdom, and in the Soviet Union the Supreme Soviet, the country's highest legislative authority, endorsed the document. One of the first major crises before the United Nations was only five years in the future with the North Korean invasion of neighbouring South Korea on June 25, 1950.

Meanwhile, the organisation had already stepped into the turmoil of the Middle East, deploying military observers and peacekeeping troops in May 1948 to monitor the armistice settled between the new nation of Israel and the surrounding Arab countries. In 1956, another troop deployment took place during the Suez Crisis to supervise the withdrawal of British, French and Israeli forces from Egypt.

Left: Soon to be familiar across the globe, the symbol of the United Nations is emblazoned on the cover page of the organisation's charter. (United Nations Public Domain via Wikimedia Commons)

Top: The Australian delegation to the United Nations Conference in San Francisco in 1945 pauses for a photograph. (Government of Australia via Wikimedia Commons)

The United Nations General Assembly addresses issues in the Middle East in the autumn of 1947. (US Government via Wikimedia Commons)

TRIAL OF GENERAL YAMASHITA BEGINS

General Tomoyuki Yamashita demands the surrender of the British garrison at Singapore in February 1942. (Collections of the Imperial War Museums via Wikimedia Commons)

Japanese General Tomoyuki Yamashita was put on trial for his life by an American military tribunal in Manila, the shattered capital of the Philippine Islands. The proceedings were destined to last from October 29 through December 7, 1945, and centred on the litany of atrocities committed by Japanese troops under Yamashita's command during World War Two in the Pacific.

On December 8, 1941, Yamashita had launched an attack on British Malaya from bases in Japanese-occupied Indochina. The mission was predicated on speed and the growing Japanese superiority in jungle warfare. With only 30,000 troops, Yamashita's 25th Army was heavily outnumbered by the British and Commonwealth defenders on the Malay peninsula, but progress was swift. Many soldiers rode bicycles, and when the tyres were flat they rode on the rims. The Japanese moved rapidly towards the British fortress of Singapore, and though the campaign had taken a toll on his forces, Yamashita convinced General Arthur Percival to surrender the garrison of 80,000 troops in the largest capitulation in British military history.

After appointment to northern China in July 1942 and promotion to full general in the summer of 1944, Yamashita, having earned the nickname 'Tiger of Malaya', was reassigned to command the defenders of the Philippines against an upcoming American invasion. He took command of the 14th Army in October just ten days before US troops landed on the island of Leyte. Further American landings occurred to the north at Lingayen Gulf in early 1945, and the Japanese were forced into the rugged mountains of Luzon to carry on a protracted resistance effort.

Meanwhile, Yamashita was hopeful that Manila would be abandoned rather than destroyed in a bitter fight. However, he had virtually no control over the city's garrison under direct command of Admiral Sanji Iwabuchi, who chose to fight. Manila was devastated, and thousands of civilian casualties were attributed to the fanatical Japanese.

On September 2, 1945, Yamashita surrendered at Kiangan on Luzon. Swiftly, he was charged with war crimes related to the fighting

Above left: In this photo from November 1945, General Yamashita is shown at centre during his war crimes trial in Manila. (National Archives and Records Administration via Wikimedia Commons)

Above right: General Tomoyuki Yamashita, the 'Tiger of Malaya', was put on trial for war crimes in the Philippines, October 29, 1945. (Government of Japan via Wikimedia Commons)

in Malaya and the Philippines. Although evidence supported the contention that he was not directly involved in the killing of civilians and prisoners of war along with other atrocities, it became clear that he also did little to curb the unnecessary bloodshed when he had the opportunity. He testified that he had no knowledge of such activities and would have issued orders to cease had he been aware.

Yamashita was found guilty and sentenced to death by hanging. General Douglas MacArthur reviewed the proceedings and found no mitigating circumstances. Further appeals were denied and President Harry Truman declined to intervene. The sentence was carried out on February 23, 1946, at the Philippine Detention and Rehabilitation Centre near Manila.

GERMANS HANGED FOR RÜSSELSHEIM MASSACRE

The town of Rüsselsheim, Germany, was the scene of a barbaric attack on American prisoners in 1944. (Creative Commons Toksave via Wikimedia Commons)

Five German civilians, including an air raid warden, were hanged for the killings of six US Army Air Forces prisoners being marched through the town of Rüsselsheim, Germany, on August 26, 1944, after their Consolidated B-24 Liberator bomber had been shot down two days earlier by heavy anti-aircraft fire during a raid on an enemy airfield.

The condemned were executed in a prison in Bruchsal, Germany, although the sentences of two women implicated in the murders were commuted to 30 years in prison rather than death. In 1947, yet another German was arrested, convicted and executed for participating in the crime.

The sad saga began on August 24, 1944, when the B-24 nicknamed 'Wham! Bam! Thank You Ma'am' of the 854th Bomb Squadron, 491st Bombardment Group, US Eighth Air Force, piloted by 2nd Lieutenant Norman J Rogers Jr, was hit by flak. The entire crew, gunners Sergeant Elmore Austin, Sergeant Sidney Brown, Staff Sergeant Forrest Brininstool, Sergeant William Dumont and Sergeant William Adams, radio operator Staff Sergeant Thomas Williams, navigator and bombardier Flight Officer Haigus Tufenkjian, co-pilot 2nd Lieutenant John Sekul, and Rogers, parachuted to earth safely. However, Brininstool was seriously wounded.

German patrols rounded up the downed airmen and took them to the town hall in Greven, Germany, and then to a nearby airfield where they spent the night. Brininstool was transported to a hospital to undergo abdominal surgery and remained there. The next day, the prisoners were placed on a train to a POW camp. At every stop they were harassed by angry mobs of civilians. During the night, Royal Air Force bombers struck the Opel manufacturing facility in Rüsselsheim, inflicting heavy damage on the town and tearing up the railroad tracks.

When the American prisoners continued their journey on foot, they were guarded by just two German soldiers. When they reached the streets of Rüsselsheim, an angry mob assembled, mistakenly

Air raid warden Josef Hartgen is led to the gallows for murdering American prisoners, November 10, 1945. (US Department of Defense via Wikimedia Commons)

believing these were the airmen responsible for destroying much of their town. Two women screamed for the Americans to be beaten to death. One of them threw a brick at the prisoners, triggering violence. Two Opel factory workers beat the defenceless men with iron rods. Air raid warden Josef Hartgen produced a pistol and shot six of the bloodied Americans in the head, killing them. Two others managed to crawl away and hide for four days before being discovered and taken to a POW camp.

When US Army troops occupied Rüsselsheim in 1945, the bodies of the murder victims were recovered on June 28. Hartgen and the others were quickly arrested, tried and convicted. A seventh man was later sentenced to death, but his conviction was overturned on a technicality. One defendant received 15 years in prison. The two women were paroled in 1953.

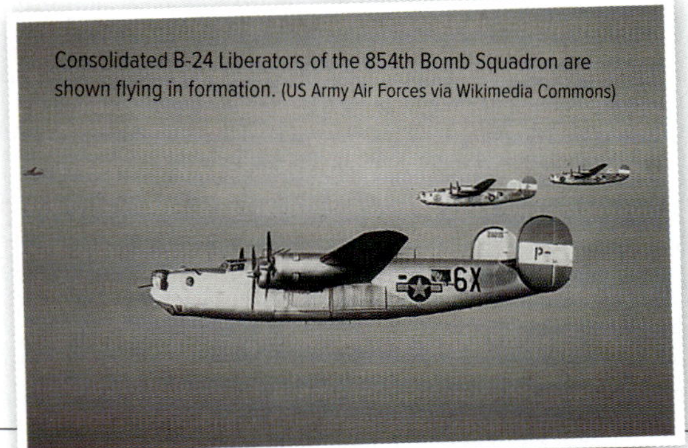

Consolidated B-24 Liberators of the 854th Bomb Squadron are shown flying in formation. (US Army Air Forces via Wikimedia Commons)

DE GAULLE ELECTED FRENCH HEAD OF STATE

Charles de Gaulle sits at centre in 1945 with members of the provisional government of France. (European Union via Wikimedia Commons)

Charles de Gaulle was elected President of the Provisional Government of the French Republic by unanimous vote of the recently established Constituent Assembly.

De Gaulle, a general of the French Army, had emerged during World War Two as the leader of the Free French movement, refusing to co-operate with the Nazis and fleeing to Britain in 1940 as the Germans overran his country. The succeeding French Vichy government, under Marshal Philippe Pétain, sentenced de Gaulle to death in absentia. However, he was not silent and issued the Appeal of June 18 over BBC radio, asking the French people and members of the armed forces then at large to rally to him.

For many, de Gaulle maintained the honour of France with his anti-Nazi movement, and he strove also to preserve the prestige of France among nations, emphasising the will to resist the Germans and contribute to the war effort even as his nation was occupied and the puppet Vichy government had engaged in collaboration.

The provisional government of France was established on June 3, 1944, and remained in place until the establishment of the Fourth Republic in October 1946. It succeeded the French Committee of National Liberation, formed as the wartime government of the country and its territories overseas were retained, and supporting the Free French movement.

In the meantime, de Gaulle became the national leader of France through action in military opposition to the Nazis and force of character. His political acumen and drive to preserve France among the most relevant of nations created some friction and mistrust between himself and US President Franklin D Roosevelt and British Prime Minister Winston Churchill. However, in time both leaders acknowledged his primacy among the political figures in France.

In October 1945, elections were held to form an expanded Constituent Assembly to draft a constitution for the Fourth Republic. A month later, de Gaulle was unanimously chosen as head of state. However, the political situation in France was fractious amid infighting and rhetoric. De Gaulle favoured a strong French presidency, but major political parties opposed the concentration of significant power in one man. The Communists were particularly restless and sought wider representation in key ministerial posts despite de Gaulle's desire to curb their influence as he suspected their greater allegiance was to the Soviet government in Moscow.

De Gaulle threatened to resign on more than one occasion and served only until January 1946, when he left office with the false expectation that his status as a national hero would spur the French people to demand his immediate return to power. Still, he remained a prominent political figure and was elected president 12 years later in 1958.

Photographed in 1942, General Charles de Gaulle led the Free French movement and maintained his country's honour. (US Government via Wikimedia Commons)

Charles de Gaulle pictured during a 1941 BBC radio address to the French people. (European Union via Wikimedia Commons)

NUREMBERG TRIALS UNDER WAY

The International Military Tribunal convenes in the Palace of Justice in Nuremberg. (National Archives and Records Administration via Wikimedia Commons)

Nazi defendants sit in the prisoners' dock during the proceedings at Nuremberg. (US Army via Wikimedia Commons)

The Allied International Military Tribunal convened in the Palace of Justice in Nuremberg, a city once steeped in the arrogance and sinister pageantry of the Nazi party. Judges of the four major Allied powers – the United States, Great Britain, Soviet Union and France – presided over the sessions that placed 24 high-ranking former Nazi officials on trial.

The tribunal itself was unprecedented in history. Its purpose was to present to the world the evidence against these accused sponsors and willing participants in heinous activities that marked the 12 years of the Third Reich, including "planning, initiating and waging of aggressive war". The accused were further being held accountable for crimes against humanity, crimes against peace, conspiracy to commit crimes against peace, and war crimes.

During the opening hours, the prosecution outlined its compelling case. The waging of systematic genocide against European Jewry and other minorities, including gypsies, homosexuals, Jehovah's Witnesses, political opponents within and outside Germany, Slavs, and more. These criminal activities were linked to forced deportation, slave labour and exploitation of resources in the occupied territories. During the proceedings, graphic films titled *The Nazi Plan* and *Nazi Concentration and Prison Camps,* depicting the horrors of the death camps, were shown. Survivors testified as to the atrocities endured and the terror of the Nazi oppression.

Chief among the defendants was former Luftwaffe leader and high-ranking Nazi Hermann Göring, who presented a challenging figure on the witness stand, particularly while refusing to admit to his direct orders to SS Obergruppenführer Reinhard Heydrich for the implementation of the "Final Solution to the Jewish Question in Europe".

Although various defendants conceded that some atrocities occurred, their counsel at times reverted to a flimsy explanation that the Nazi leaders were simply following orders.

The Nuremberg trials concluded on October 1, 1946, with 12 defendants found guilty and sentenced to death. Three others received life in prison, and some received long prison terms of up to 20 years. The Nuremberg trials are remembered not only for adjudicating the cases of top Nazis, but also for establishing the tenets of individual responsibility for illegal activities directed by a state government.

Although Göring cheated the hangman by ingesting cyanide, ten convicted individuals were hanged, beginning at 1.10am on October 16, 1946, in the gymnasium of their Nuremberg prison, where three temporary gallows had been erected. Those sentenced to prison terms were transferred to Spandau Prison in Berlin. Convicted of crimes against peace, former Deputy Führer Rudolf Hess was the longest-serving Spandau inmate, spending 40 years behind bars from 1946 until his death by apparent suicide in 1987.

Former Deputy Führer Rudolf Hess served 40 years at Spandau Prison prior to his apparent suicide in 1987. (Creative Commons Bundesarchiv Bild via Wikimedia Commons)

EZRA POUND ARRAIGNED FOR TREASON

Famed American poet, literary critic and political theorist Ezra Pound was arraigned on charges of treason, in Washington DC. The original indictment was issued by a grand jury on July 26, 1943, while Pound and his wife Dorothy were living in Italy.

Pound was a well-known member of the literary community and was familiar with many luminaries. In the 1920s, he edited the T S Eliot classic *The Waste Land* after providing a glowing review of Eliot's classic poem *The Love Song of J Alfred Prufrock* several years earlier. He also contributed to the rise in popularity of such authors as James Joyce, Robert Frost and Ernest Hemingway, while his own works included *Ripostes, Hugh Selwyn Mauberley* and *The Cantos*, an epic written across decades from 1917 to 1962.

Pound was not only remembered as a poet and literary critic, but also as a mentally unstable Fascist propagandist during World War Two who espoused contempt for the Jewish race and lambasted President Franklin D Roosevelt during a series of radio broadcasts in the war years that originated in Italy and were aired from January 1941 through March 1945. Pound was an admirer of Nazi Germany and Führer Adolf Hitler as well as Fascist Italy and dictator Benito Mussolini. The expatriate Pound left the United States in 1907, living in London and Paris before relocating to Italy in 1924, two years after Mussolini's rise to power, and resided in the town of Rapallo on the Ligurian Riviera for the next 20 years.

With the outbreak of World War Two, Pound initiated a campaign of letter writing to American political figures, telling one senator: "I have read a regulation that only those foreigners are to be admitted to the US who are deemed to be useful... the dirtiest Jews from Paris..?"

In March 1942, Pound ranted over the radio: "You let in the Jew and the Jew rotted your empire..."

The United States Foreign Broadcast Monitoring Service recorded evidence of Pound's treasonous broadcasts, which led to his 1943 indictment in absentia. On May 3, 1944, Pound was arrested by Italian partisans. He was turned over to the US Counter Intelligence Corps in Genoa and transferred to the US Army Disciplinary Training Center near Pisa on the 24th. He arrived in Washington DC on November 18 and within days was declared mentally unfit to stand trial. Pound was taken to St Elizabeth's Hospital, where he was held for 12 years.

After his release in 1958, Pound returned to Italy and spent the remainder of his life there. He died in Venice at the age of 87 on November 1, 1972.

Right: Treasonous poet Ezra Pound was living in Europe when this passport photo was taken in 1919. (US Government via Wikimedia Commons)

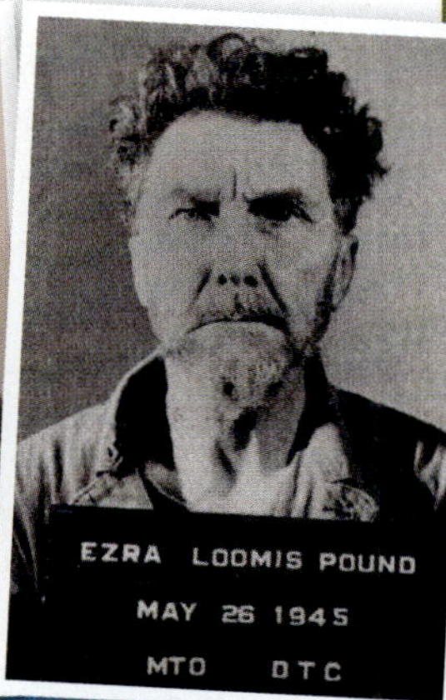

Far right: This prison photo of Ezra Pound was taken while in the custody of US authorities in Italy. (US Government via Wikimedia Commons)

Unfit for trial, Ezra Pound was held in St Elizabeth's Hospital in Washington DC as a mental patient for 12 years. (Creative Commons Tom via Wikimedia Commons)

FASCIST JOHN AMERY PLEADS GUILTY

A couple of recruits to the pro-Nazi British Legion of St George, later the British Free Corps, are shown in German Waffen-SS uniforms. (Government of the United Kingdom via Wikimedia Commons)

Fascist sympathisers. He chose to remain in France after the Nazi military victory in the spring of 1940, living under the Vichy government before visiting Germany in the autumn of 1942. At that time, Amery suggested the formation of a British force that would fight alongside the Wehrmacht. Meanwhile, he made numerous pro-Nazi propaganda radio broadcasts.

When Amery began actively recruiting his so-called British Legion of St George, he visited a POW camp in occupied France and appealed to the captives to join him in the proposed Waffen-SS unit. The response was dismal and eventually the idea was dropped. Amery remained in Berlin and continued his pro-Nazi activities before travelling to northern Italy in 1944. He was taken prisoner by Italian partisans along with his mistress, Michelle Thomas, in April 1945, and narrowly averted summary execution. Subsequently, he was turned over to British authorities and brought to London aboard an aircraft along with William Joyce, the propagandist nicknamed "Lord Haw Haw".

Following his guilty plea, Amery was hanged at Wandsworth Prison on December 19, 1945. He was 33 years old.

Right: The Right Honourable Sir Travers Humphreys, shown soon after being called to the bar in the late 19th century. He pronounced sentence against traitor John Amery. (United Kingdom Work by a Crown Agency Public Domain via Wikimedia Commons)

Below: Traitor John Amery entered a guilty plea to charges of treason and was hanged in December 1945. (Bassano Ltd Public Domain via Wikimedia Commons)

Although he had previously argued that he was not a Nazi, but an anti-Communist, and that he had never directly opposed Great Britain, Fascist and Nazi sympathiser John Amery pleaded guilty before a judge at the Old Bailey to eight counts of high treason and treachery. In addition to his own prior argument, Amery's legal counsel and family members, including his father Leo Amery – former First Lord of the Admiralty, Member of Parliament and Secretary of State for the Colonies and for India and Burma – pleaded that he was mentally ill and incapable of standing trial.

The earlier court proceedings were rendered moot as John Amery abruptly departed from previous tactics on the first day of his trial and entered the guilty plea. The session required only eight minutes, and before accepting Amery's admission of guilt, the Right Honourable Sir Travers Humphreys, presiding, satisfied himself that Amery understood its implications. There was only one sentence to be imposed – death.

Humphreys pronounced sentence and commented: "I have read the depositions and the exhibits in this case, and I am satisfied that you knew what you did and that you did it intentionally and deliberately after you had received warning from more than one of your fellow countrymen that the course you were pursuing amounted to high treason. They called you a traitor and you heard them; but in spite of that you continued in that course. You now stand a self-confessed traitor to your King and country, and you have forfeited your right to live."

Amery had been a troubled child and grown into a right-wing advocate for the Nationalists under Generalissimo Francisco Franco during the Spanish Civil War and subsequently resided in France in company with other

HOMMA TRIAL ORDERED TO PROCEED

General Masaharu Homma posed for this portrait during the Japanese occupation of the Philippines. (Government of Japan via Wikimedia Commons)

General Masaharu Homma testifies in his own defence during his war crimes trial of 1946. (US Army Signal Corps via Wikimedia Commons)

General Douglas MacArthur, Supreme Commander of the Allied Powers and military governor of Japan, ordered the trial of Japanese General Masaharu Homma to proceed. Homma, arrested in Japan in September 1945, was returned to the Philippines to answer to an indictment of 48 counts of violating the international rules of war.

The charges were the result of the horrific Bataan Death March that followed the Japanese 14th Army's conquest of the Philippines while under Homma's command. With the surrender of the last American and Filipino resistance at the Bataan peninsula and the island of Corregidor, the Japanese had anticipated around 25,000 prisoners. The total actually rose to 78,000, and no provision had been made to feed, house and provide medical care for such an overwhelming number. The Japanese had also suffered heavily during the Philippine campaign and were not inclined to stretch available resources to accommodate prisoners.

General Masaharu Homma discusses the surrender of American and Filipino troops on Bataan with American General Jonathan M Wainwright. (Government of Japan via Wikimedia Commons)

The infamous Bataan Death March, conducted April 9-17, 1942, was punctuated with Japanese atrocities. Many of the prisoners were ill, malnourished and deprived of water. Those who broke ranks to drink from a fetid puddle or collapsed due to exhaustion were regularly shot on the spot or beheaded. The trek from Bataan to the prison of Camp O'Donnell on the island of Luzon covered about 65 torturous miles amid stifling heat, and estimates of the dead vary widely. Fatalities are believed to have exceeded 10,000.

Homma had previously earned a reputation as a commander who cared about his troops, unwilling to sacrifice their lives for a speedier campaign in the Philippines. He further attempted to convince his superiors to treat the Filipino people as friends rather than a conquered and subservient population. Such conduct gained the enmity of both superior officers and subordinates, and he was relieved of command in June 1942 due to his leniency toward civilians and prisoners alike. He spent the remainder of the war in relative obscurity in Japan.

Homma's trial began in Manila on January 3, 1946, and he was reportedly shocked by the evidence presented. Asserting that he had no knowledge of the atrocities committed, he told the court: "I am horrified to learn these things happened under my command. I am ashamed of our troops."

The trial raised questions regarding the responsibility of commanders for the conduct of their subordinate troops, and even though witnesses testified on Homma's behalf, the harrowing accounts of the Death March made conviction inevitable. The outcome of the trial remains a subject of legal debate to this day. Homma was found guilty and executed by firing squad, a death considered more honourable than hanging, at Los Banos on April 3, 1946.

GENERAL PATTON INJURED IN AUTO ACCIDENT

Pallbearers carry the coffin of General George S Patton Jr to his final resting place, December 24, 1945. (US Army Signal Corps via Wikimedia Commons)

One of the most controversial and successful field commanders of World War Two in Europe, General George S Patton Jr, was seriously injured in an automobile accident in Germany en route to a hunting excursion. Patton was hospitalised and succumbed to his injuries 12 days later.

Throughout the war in Europe, Patton had been a notable figure. A pioneer of the US Army's armoured forces between the world wars and an advocate of swift, mobile ground warfare, he assumed high command with America's entry into the conflict. He was devoutly religious, foul-mouthed and believed in reincarnation while wearing a pair of ivory-handled pistols as sidearms. A stickler for military protocol, he frequently upbraided soldiers for being out of uniform or slacking.

During Operation Torch, the Allied invasion of North Africa on November 8, 1942, Patton commanded the Western Task Force, which landed at Casablanca, Morocco. In Operation Husky, the July 1943 invasion of Sicily, Patton commanded the US Seventh Army, landing at Gela. He chafed at the supporting role assigned in protecting the flank of the British Eighth Army, under General Bernard Montgomery, fighting its way towards the port of Messina. Substantially on his own initiative, Patton ordered US troops to take the city of Palermo and then drive to Messina ahead of Montgomery. A bitter rivalry ensued between the two mercurial leaders, lasting through the end of the war in western Europe.

Meanwhile, Patton visited medical facilities in Sicily and slapped two soldiers being treated for combat fatigue. The incidents were widely reported in the media and Patton was reprimanded by his longtime friend and superior officer General Dwight D Eisenhower. He was sidelined during the preparations for the Allied invasion of French Normandy on June 6, 1944, and was instead a decoy, heading the fictitious First US Army Group (FUSAG) in Operation Fortitude, the successful effort to convince the Nazis that the invasion would occur at the Pas de Calais rather than Normandy.

At long last, Patton re-entered active combat command with the activation of the Third Army and executed a brilliant run across

The grave of General George S Patton Jr at the American Military Cemetery in Hamm, Luxembourg, is visited annually by thousands. (US Army via Wikimedia Commons)

General Patton (right) watches American troop movements in North Africa with General Terry Allen (centre) and General Theodore Roosevelt Jr, March 1943. (Robert Capa Public Domain via Wikimedia Commons)

General Patton smokes a pipe while observing US Army manoeuvres in Louisiana in 1941. (US Army via Wikimedia Commons)

France following Operation Cobra, the breakout from the Normandy beachhead. His momentum was substantially slowed by lack of fuel and supplies, and the rivalry with Montgomery gained new ardour. During the Battle of the Bulge in December 1944, Patton executed an outstanding manoeuvre, disengaging from a winter battle in the Saar and pivoting northward to relieve the besieged garrison of the vital crossroads town of Bastogne, Belgium.

After the war in Europe ended, Patton was hopeful of receiving a battlefield command in the Pacific. However, he realised that such an assignment was unlikely. Instead, he was installed as military governor of Bavaria. In this role, his controversial comments regarding the new world order after the Allied victory, the future of relations with the Soviet Union and the Allied policy of rapid de-Nazification resulted in his relief from command of the Third Army. His pragmatic approach to the administration of the Bavarian government led him to conclude that the continued use of some former Nazi party members was essential in keeping the switchboards working, deliveries of mail and the operation of public transportation. Therefore, he declined to participate fully in the wholesale dismissal of former Nazis from vital roles.

When Eisenhower had had enough of the controversy, he placed Patton in charge of the Fifteenth Army, which was engaged in writing a history of the recent war, at Bad Nauheim, Germany.

Patton was deeply depressed following his relief from Third Army command, and his chief of staff, General Hobart Gay, arranged a pheasant hunt near the town of Speyer, Germany, hoping to lift his commanding officer's spirits. While travelling to the site on the morning of December 9, 1945, Patton's 1938 Cadillac Model 75 limousine was involved in an accident when the driver of an army truck turned left in front of the general's vehicle.

General Gay and the driver were only slightly injured, but General Patton was thrown violently forward. He struck the overhead light and the steel partition inside the Cadillac, suffering a broken nose while a large swath of his scalp was peeled back from his forehead. He bled profusely. He was rushed to the 130th Station Hospital in Heidelberg,

Germany, where x-rays revealed the worst injury. The fractures of cervical vertebrae three and four had damaged the spinal cord resulting in paralysis from the neck down.

Although doctors were initially optimistic that Patton would survive, his condition deteriorated, and he died of pulmonary oedema and congestive heart failure at the age of 60 on December 21, 1945. Following a funeral in Luxembourg City, the general was interred in the American Military Cemetery at Hamm, Luxembourg, on December 24, after previously expressing his wish to be buried among the soldiers he had led to glory during World War Two.

A quarter of a century after his death, the story of General Patton was brought to the silver screen in the major motion picture *Patton*, starring actor George C Scott, who received the 1970 Academy Award for Best Actor. A new generation became familiar with the life and times of one of the most successful, but controversial figures in American military history.

An early advocate for the development of armoured formations in the US Army, Patton stands before a French tank in 1918. (National Archives and Records Administration via Wikimedia Commons)

Generals Patton and Montgomery shake hands in Sicily during their heated rivalry. (US Army via Wikimedia Commons)

FUMIMARO KONOE COMMITS SUICIDE

Above: Prince Fumimaro Konoe stands in the foreground with members of his cabinet, July 1941. Government of Japan via Wikimedia Commons)

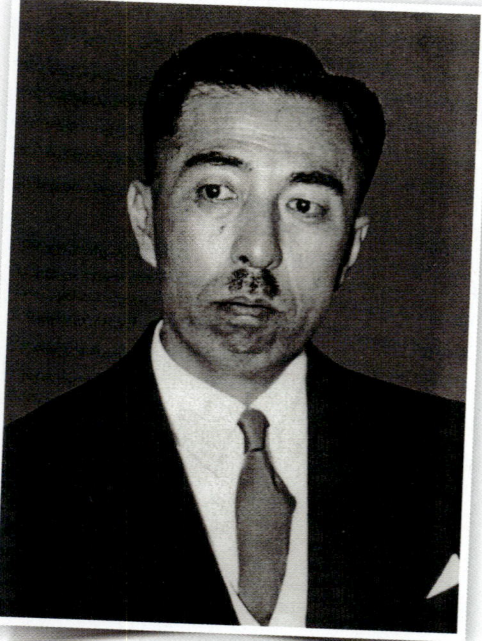

Left: Former Prime Minister of Japan Prince Fumimaro Konoe committed suicide rather than face imprisonment and trial for war crimes. Government of Japan via Wikimedia Commons)

Prince Fumimaro Konoe, former two-term prime minister of Japan, committed suicide by ingesting cyanide rather than submitting to captivity in Tokyo's Sugamo Prison and facing trial for war crimes.

In recent months, Konoe had played a key role in toppling the regime of Prime Minister Hideki Tojo, a vehement war hawk, following the fall of the Marianas to the Americans. He had further implored Emperor Hirohito to seek peace talks to end World War Two in the Pacific, but his entreaties had fallen on deaf ears. After the war in the Pacific ended, Konoe served in the first post-war Japanese government but came under suspicion for war crimes.

Konoe had ascended to the office of prime minister in 1937 and presided over much of the Japanese military expansion in China and the nation's evolution to a totalitarian state. However, it must be stated that the aggression of the Japanese Kwantung Army in China was driven largely by the military itself while the Tokyo government was virtually powerless to curb the adventurism. The litany of atrocities committed by Japanese troops against innocent Chinese civilians was horrific and included the infamous Rape of Nanking from December 1937 to January 1938, during which thousands of innocent people were murdered.

During both terms as prime minister, Konoe sought to restrict Japanese militarism to the Chinese campaign and thereby avert war with the West, particularly the United States. His second term in office ended on October 18, 1941, just weeks before the Japanese attack on Pearl Harbor. When he heard of the attack, Konoe remarked: "What on earth? I really feel a miserable defeat coming…" His efforts to avoid war had been largely impeded by Tojo, then serving as War Minister and bent on widening the war in the Pacific.

Succeeded by Tojo as prime minister in 1941, Konoe faded temporarily from the halls of political power in Tokyo. His re-emergence was then marked by the continuing effort to seek peace.

On the night before his suicide, Konoe and his son, Michitaka, discussed the years of intervention and conquest in China, the failed effort to avoid war with the United States and the responsibility the former prime minister had shouldered for Emperor Hirohito and the Japanese people. Konoe believed that the charge of war crimes and humiliation of a public trial were more than he could bear. American historian and author John Toland later wrote that the two sat in silence and the son asked if his father would in fact go to prison the following day. There was no reply.

Konoe's lifeless body was found by his wife the next morning.

Prince Konoe and his cabinet pose for a photo in July 1940. Hideki Tojo stands behind and to his right. Government of Japan via Wikimedia Commons)

CONCLUSION

The year 1945 was a watershed in human history. The most destructive conflict ever imagined had become reality and then, after agonising loss of life and resources, came to an end with a thunderous event whose magnitude reverberates around the world today.

Lives and memories are measured with the end of World War Two. It holds an immovable place, and events are remembered in their proximity before and afterwards. So 1945 marks a boundary between the old and new, what living was like and what it would become.

That thunderous event was the dawn of the Atomic Age and the realisation that mankind could destroy itself in the blink of an eye. During his final statement before the International Military Tribunal at Nuremberg, Albert Speer, Hitler's architect and Minister of Armaments, alluded to that terrible awareness.

Speer said: "This war ended with remote-controlled rockets, aircraft travelling at the speed of sound, new types of submarines, torpedoes

The Big Three – Churchill, Roosevelt and Stalin – pause during the Yalta Conference in February 1945; even then their alliance, East and West, was tenuous. (US Army Signal Corps via Wikimedia Commons)

After World War Two ended, the Führerbunker where Hitler spent his last delirious days was demolished in the removal of vestiges of the Nazi era. (Creative Commons Bundesarchiv Bild via Wikimedia Commons)

which find their own target, with atom bombs and with the prospect of a horrible kind of chemical warfare.

"Of necessity, the next war will be overshadowed by these new destructive inventions of the human mind. In five or ten years the technique of warfare will make it possible to fire rockets from continent to continent with uncanny precision. By atomic power it can destroy one million people in the centre of New York in a matter of seconds with a rocket operated, perhaps by only ten men, invisible, without previous warning, faster than sound, by day and by night. Science is able to spread pestilence among human beings and animals and to destroy crops by insect warfare. Chemistry has developed

Soldiers of the 15th Scottish Division cross the Rhine during Operation Plunder. (Collections of the Imperial War Museums via Wikimedia Commons)

US Marines fight the Japanese on Okinawa, taking cover behind the tombstones of Cemetery Ridge, June 1, 1945. (Creative Commons, Archives Branch US Marine Corps History Division via Wikimedia Commons)

women and children while their villages went up in flames, to the gas chambers and the plague of emotionally detached armed forces spreading destruction in their conquering path. A sense of superiority led the Japanese to impose the Greater East Asia Co-prosperity Sphere on the rest of the region. Although it was presented for propaganda purposes as a cleansing of Western influence so that Asia would be for Asians, in reality it was intended as Asia for the Japanese. The Rape of Nanking, the slaughter of civilian populations and the brutal treatment of prisoners of war in the Bataan Death March made the real root of Japanese aggression plain.

All this was brought into the harsh, 'cleansing' light of day in 1945.

And then there was the spawn of divisive ideology, a clash of visions for the post-war world. The Allied powers, East and West, had fought and defeated the common Axis enemy. But beyond that lay the spheres of influence, the establishment of governments that were "friendly", of power across the globe amid the emergence of the Third World as empires were rapidly dismantled.

The seeds of the Cold War were sown on the battlefields and in the conference rooms of World War Two; the contentious nature of the next half a century was made apparent in the events of 1945.

terrible weapons with which it can inflict unspeakable suffering upon helpless human beings."

An accompaniment to Speer's ominous observance, laid bare to the world in 1945, was the depth of man's inhumanity to man. The collective brutality of so-called civilised nations brought another dimension to the scope of human depravity. The Germans were historically a cultured and learned people. They had been beguiled by the rhetoric, rapt by the contagious hysteria, and led to utter destruction by the twisted vision of an Aryan race and the madness of Adolf Hitler. Benito Mussolini had roused the Italian people with dreams of restoring the glory of ancient Rome. The Japanese people had been stirred to conquer Asia and the Pacific because of their inherent belief in their superiority to other peoples, other races – they saw in their opponents an inherent weakness that would surely cause them to be vanquished on the battlefield.

The genocide against those the Nazis deemed Untermensch, the racially and socially inferior, led to the concentration camps and the merciless persecution of European Jewry and other groups, to the death squads that haunted the steppes of Russia and summarily shot

Sailors strain to view the moment of the Japanese surrender aboard the battleship USS *Missouri*, September 2, 1945. (US Navy via Wikimedia Commons)

Allied military commanders including Soviet Marshal Georgy Zhukov and British Field Marshal Bernard Montgomery walk before the Brandenburg Gate in Berlin. (Library and Archives of Canada via Wikimedia Commons)

Despite the glimmer of hope and the commitment to lasting peace around the world that the birth of the United Nations represented, there was no escaping the conclusion that the Superpowers – the United States and the Soviet Union – were destined to collide in the political arena and in proxy wars across the globe. Then, only four years after Hiroshima and Nagasaki, the Soviets detonated their first atomic bomb. Ideological, political, nationalistic and territorial perspectives were prosecuted against the backdrop of a nuclear arms race.

The legacy of World War Two and its culmination in 1945, therefore, has been lived in the halls of the United Nations and on the floor of its General Assembly, in conflicts in China, Korea, Vietnam and the Middle East, in the Cuban Missile Crisis, in Afghanistan and Iraq and even today in Ukraine.

Peace remains elusive. But hope remains, too. It remains in the lessons of 1945.